TREES
FOR THE SMALL
GARDEN

TREES
FOR THE SMALL
GARDEN

How to choose, plant, and care for the tree that
makes the garden special

Simon Toomer

Timber Press
Portland • Cambridge

A Quarto Book

Published in 2005 by
Timber Press, Inc.
The Haseltine Building
133 S.W. Second Avenue,
Suite 450, Portland,
Oregon 97204-3527,
U.S.A

Timber Press
2 Station Road
Swavesey
Cambridge
CB4 5QJ
UK

www.timberpress.com

ISBN 0-88192-683-3

Catalog records for this book are available
from the Library of Congress and the
British Library.

QUAR.TREE

Conceived, designed, and produced by
Quarto Publishing plc
The Old Brewery
6 Blundell Street
London N7 9BH

Project Editor: Liz Pasfield
Art Editor: Anna Knight
Copy Editor: Sue Viccars
Designer: Brian Flynn
Assistant Art Director: Penny Cobb
Photographer: Steve Wooster
Picture Research: Claudia Tate
Illustrator: Kuo Kang Chen
Proofreader: Sally MacEachern
Indexer: Pamela Ellis

Art Director: Moira Clinch
Publisher: Piers Spence

Color separation by Provision Pte Ltd,
Singapore
Printed by SNP Leefung Ltd in China

9 8 7 6 5 4 3 2 1

Contents

Why a tree?

Planting trees is one of the most valuable and enduring things we can do, and can be carried out quickly, cheaply, and without any specialist equipment. Fortunately, trees are not as slow growing as is commonly supposed and the rewards of today's planting can be enjoyed by the planter as well as the following generations. Nowhere is this truer than in small gardens where even a modestly sized tree can have an impact within only a few years of planting, and carry on developing and maturing for decades.

Nowadays we have an unprecedented choice of trees from all over the world with which to decorate our gardens. As well as their purely aesthetic values they still have a functional role in our lives, in particular helping to soften some of the negative aspects of the urban environment, dampening unwelcome noise, screening unsightly development, and providing shade and shelter. As well as giving height and structure, their gradual development and longevity add an element of stability not provided by herbaceous plants. They also have the capacity to modify the garden climate, allowing a greater range of less hardy plants to thrive in the protection they provide. Many species acquire great character with age, becoming an integral part of a house and garden and even adding to their value.

It should not be forgotten that as well as the many positive contributions made by garden trees, when used badly they are one of the commonest causes of dispute between neighbors. Inappropriate planting of fast-growing conifers such as Leyland cypress has led to some governments introducing legislation to counter the problem, and huge sums of money are spent annually by local authorities and homeowners in a never-ending battle to control overgrown trees. Insurance claims resulting from subsidence damage to buildings has risen sharply in many areas, and trees are often to blame. Such problems get urban trees a bad name and underline the importance of careful selection and positioning if they are to be an asset rather than a cause of expense and dispute. This book is intended to help those faced with the bewildering array of trees available to make the right choice for their particular circumstances.

Careful selection and planting of trees like Salix daphnoides *(left) can provide all-year interest.*

Tree or shrub?

There is no universally agreed distinction between a tree and a shrub. Both produce a woody skeleton of stems and branches that allows them to grow larger than herbaceous plants to compete for sunlight. We usually think of trees as bigger and with more of a tendency to grow from a single stem. Shrubs, on the other hand, have many stems and are usually smaller. In the context of a garden it is useful to think in terms of landscape, with trees as the largest plants providing a canopy above the smaller shrubs and herbaceous plants below, just as they do in natural forests. Many of the plants included in this book could qualify as trees or shrubs but, given suitable conditions and perhaps a little judicious pruning, all have the potential to make a small tree and play that role in the garden.

The small garden

We all have our own idea of what constitutes a small garden, based on our own experience. What would be considered large in an urban setting may be thought very modest by suburban or rural standards. For that reason, this book does not set out to precisely define the small garden. Rather, the aim has been to select trees small enough to be suitable for a range of domestic situations. In a sense, all domestic gardens are small compared to large municipal and private gardens, and the important thing is to choose plants that will be in scale with their surroundings.

The featured trees

The list of trees featured is a small selection of those available. It represents a broad spectrum of plants to provide enough choice to meet the tree needs of all but the most particular of gardeners. Most are well-known species, easily obtainable from general plant suppliers, while a few are included to provide something a little unusual for those with an eye for novelty. Along with the 80

main featured trees are supplementary ones that may be more suitable for some situations or provide an alternative to the more commonly seen choices. Many of the trees chosen are cultivars, varieties that have been specially selected for certain desirable characteristics such as distinctive flower color or weeping habit. For some species the list of available cultivars runs into hundreds, and only a few have been chosen as representatives.

All but a few of the trees featured can be described as small, rarely growing to a height of more than 33 ft. (10m). Many are considerably smaller and are suitable for very restricted spaces or for complementing larger trees. The growth rate and ultimate size of trees varies greatly from one place to another, and the figures given are inevitably approximations. Where larger species are included, or there is the potential for a tree to grow larger than its indicated height, this is clearly identified in the text and factfinder. A few, like *Eucalyptus gunnii* and *Salix alba*, have been included with a recommendation for regular pruning to provide ornamental foliage or shoots.

The chosen species vary greatly in their hardiness and cultural requirements. Some are very adaptable, able to grow in a broad range of conditions, while others are far choosier with specialist needs.

Most gardens have enough room for at least one specimen tree.

7

Choosing the right tree

Before going out to buy a tree for a garden, it is best to take some time considering the options. No plant center is big enough to accommodate all the available species and cultivars, and time spent looking at books and catalogs may reveal a whole new range of choice that would otherwise have been overlooked.

The most important thing to bear in mind is the situation for which the trees are intended to grow. Too often people make a hurried choice based purely on the appearance of a plant itself with no regard to its attributes, requirements, or the function it needs to fulfill in the garden. Just like the beguiling puppy in the pet store window, purchases made in haste can have long-lasting consequences, especially when that small sapling shoots to over 80 ft. (25m) and outgrows the garden. It is much better to take time to decide what the tree is wanted for so that a more objective decision can be made to match the garden's requirements to the attributes of a particular plant. The final choice may still have an element of emotional impulse, but it should at least be based on a shortlist of suitable candidates.

The first questions to ask are to do with what the tree is needed for and whether there are any particular attributes required. Once this has been determined a list of plants that meet those criteria can be drawn up. Finally, the list can be refined to include only those trees that will tolerate the particular climatic, soil, and other conditions encountered in the intended location. Factfinders and selectors are particularly useful in this process.

Although books and catalogs can provide ideas, facts, and figures, there is nothing like seeing the plant "in the flesh," and visits to botanical gardens and arboreta are invaluable for checking out selected trees before purchase.

Trees can be used in a variety of ways in the garden landscape. The irregular outline of trees like Amelanchier *(left) can provide an interesting contrast with the geometric lines of contemporary design.*

The garden landscape

Trees play a very important role in the landscape of almost all gardens. They provide the structural framework below which the smaller and more ephemeral plants can be arranged. When designing from scratch they are often the first things to be sited, but for most of us inheriting an established garden, we must, to some extent, choose trees to complement the existing features.

Whether it's an individual plant that is required to meet a particular need, or a number to provide an overall structure, it is important to consider how they will contribute to the variety of colors, textures, and shapes to create a varied and interesting atmosphere. If a garden is to be more than just a jumble of plants it is also important that they are arranged so as to complement each other and show off their attributes to the full. Seasonal plants should be chosen and positioned carefully to provide a sequence of interest and brighten up even the dullest times of the year. Whether it be flowers, stem color, or fall fruit, by careful combination it is possible to ensure that as one plant's display fades, another is about to step into the limelight. For some, like *Amelanchier*, the floral display is short-lived, and for the rest of the year it relies on the modest beauty of its foliage for appeal. Others, such as *Betula pendula* 'Youngii,' have all-year-round impact and should be given pride of place in a prominent position. In very small gardens with only enough room for a few plants, trees like this are particularly valuable. A few species are of such unusual or dramatic appearance as to make a particularly bold landscape statement. Purple-foliaged plants such as *Cotinus coggygria* 'Royal Purple,' and those with highly unusual leaves, like *Trachycarpus fortunei*, fall into this category. It is always tempting to fill the garden with plants like this in an effort to ensure constant spectacle. As in most things, you can have too much of a good thing and such a policy inevitably results in a devaluing of even the most spectacular plant. They should be used very sparingly, and most small gardens are unlikely to have room for more than one or two.

Some kinds of plants play a more supportive role in the garden. Evergreens, such as yews and hollies, may not be the most dramatic of plants in themselves, but for much of the year are the great unsung heroes of garden design, providing backgrounds to enhance more ornamental species and screens to control views. They may have an even more down-to-earth function as hedges to define boundaries, or shelter planting against cold winds.

Size

Of all the characteristics to be decided on when choosing trees, size must be the most important. As well as the obvious need to avoid species that will outgrow the garden, it is important that they are in scale with the space available and complement the other plants. Even trees that reach the modest height of about 33 ft. (10m) are too large for some spaces, while smaller individuals of 6 to 9 ft. (2 to 3m) would look out of proportion if grown as specimens in larger settings.

As well as height, spread is an important consideration. *Parrotia persica*, with a typical height of about 26 ft. (8m), may seem a better choice for a confined space than *Juniperus scopulorum* that may reach 40 ft. (12m). However, the latter's narrow form allows it to be accommodated in gardens where the spreading habit of *Parrotia* would soon become a problem.

One difficulty with predicting plants' eventual size is their great variability. Even individuals of the same species show marked differences depending on climate, soil conditions, and origin. *Magnolia grandiflora* frequently reaches a height of over 80 ft. (25m) in the southern states of the USA but is restricted to much more modest proportions when planted further north. It may be possible, particularly with more common trees, to look around in neighboring gardens to see how large a particular species is likely to get. However, if in doubt it is best to err on the side of caution and choose something smaller. Fortunately, many

cultivars have been selected that provide scaled-down versions of species. *Magnolia grandiflora* is a good example, with 'Little Gem' among its many smaller cultivars.

Hardiness and climate

Having determined the physical and aesthetic attributes needed to complement the garden landscape, it is important to ensure that the trees chosen will succeed in the climatic zone for which they are intended. Even the most beautiful species grown in unsuitable conditions can turn out to be an ugly and disappointing specimen.

Hardiness is one of the most important considerations and may impose severe limitations on the list of possible species. It is useful to refer to climate zone maps such as those at the back of this book. These provide guidance based on the minimum winter temperatures likely to be encountered in each zone, and can be used in conjunction with the figures given for each plant in the selector. However useful these are, they cannot hope to encompass the more subtle variations in conditions that occur locally and

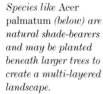

Species like Acer palmatum *(below) are natural shade-bearers and may be planted beneath larger trees to create a multi-layered landscape.*

should not be used religiously. Some plants, like *Azara microphylla*, may be grown in zones below their quoted figure with the shelter of a wall, while others that should in theory be hardy in a particular area may prove not to be due to spring frost patterns. An additional factor to bear in mind is that plants adapted to cool conditions often do less well in warmer climates. This should be considered carefully where plants are intended for zones well above their minimum.

Watering the garden is a chore that most people would prefer not to have to do. Occasional supplementary watering during dry spells is one thing, but it is best to avoid planting trees that have requirements well in excess of the natural rainfall for an average year. In dry climates it is best therefore to select trees like *Robinia pseudoacacia* 'Frisia' that have the ability to survive periods of drought. Again, selectors are useful for helping to determine which plants are suitable.

Aspect

Trees have evolved in a variety of different wild environments. *Acer palmatum*, for example, grows naturally in the forests of central China, Korea, and Japan, commonly in the partial shade of larger trees. This characteristic can be used to advantage in the garden where it can occupy shady situations or form an intermediate layer between larger trees and herbaceous plants. Some trees, on the other hand, require full sunlight if they are to thrive or flower well. Most willows are known for their dislike of shade, and *Koelreuteria paniculata* rarely flowers unless given full sunlight.

Shelter is also an important factor determining the success of some species, particularly in their young stages. Tender trees like *Embothrium* and *Crinodendron* may be grown successfully in areas outside their normal

In practice many trees, including hawthorns, grow best in climatic zones at, or a little above, their minimum and are less successful in much warmer zones.

climatic limit with the shelter of a protective wall or adjacent plants. Others such as *Stewartia* and some species of *Nyssa* benefit from shelter even within their climatic zones. Some of the most useful species are those that thrive even in quite severe exposure and can be used as windbreaks for humans and other plants alike. All species of *Crataegus* come into this category, as do most birches and pines.

Soil conditions

Like all plants, trees vary greatly in their soil requirements, and it is usually their tolerance to various adverse conditions rather than strict requirements that limits their success. When we say, for example, that a particular plant requires an acid soil, it is more accurate to say that it cannot tolerate alkaline conditions.

Soil type is a fairly loosely used term that refers to the proportions of sand and clay in the soil. This has a strong influence on its ability to retain water, drainage, and fertility. Some trees, such as pines and birches, thrive in the relatively poor, dry conditions encountered on freely drained sandy soils. Others such as *Stewartia* have more demanding tastes, requiring a moist but well-drained loamy soil. Soils that are constantly wet or liable to periodic waterlogging, particularly during the growing season, require specialist species. Willows and alders are the most obvious candidates for these conditions, but less well-known ones include *Betula pendula* and *Sorbus aucuparia*.

The pH of a soil is a measure of its acidity or alkalinity. The scale runs from 1 to 14 with 7 being neutral, and acid and alkaline being lower and higher respectively. In general, alkaline soils tend to be more fertile, but at high levels (above about 7.5) nutrients become unobtainable by many plants. This is why tolerance of high pH is such an important factor in determining the suitability of plants for lime soils. Acid soils tend to be poorer as nutrient elements are freely dissolved and leached out. In practice, alkaline soils impose a greater constraint on species choice than acid ones. However, there are plenty of species that will thrive even in quite severe alkaline conditions, and trees are often more tolerant than they are given credit for. The ultimate solution for accommodating a "must-have" tree—despite unsuitable soil conditions—is to grow it in a container with its own particular taste in compost (see "Planting trees," page 16).

Some trees are able to thrive on almost any kind of soil and provide an obvious choice where conditions are less than ideal. *Rhus typhina* is one such plant, a fact that explains its great popularity and success.

Pests and diseases

Trees suffer from a multitude of pests and diseases, requiring a specialist book to do the subject credit. Most are sporadic in distribution and occurrence and need not be considered when choosing trees for a garden. Others, such as honey fungus, are common and serious and, where established in a garden, may influence choice in favor of more resistant species.

A few diseases are sufficiently severe and prevalent to render certain trees completely

Trees vary greatly in their soil requirements and tolerances. Some, like Rhus (below left), thrive in almost any conditions, including soils far too dry for more choosy species such as Ilex aquifolium (below right).

unsuitable for some areas. An obvious example is fireblight, a bacterial disease that affects those genera of the rose family that possess apple-like fruits, including *Pyrus, Sorbus, Crataegus,* and *Malus.* As well as being very damaging to ornamental trees and shrubs, it is a commercially important disease in fruit-growing areas. Where plants susceptible to diseases such as fireblight are chosen for planting, advice on their suitability for use in a particular area should be sought from local arboricultural or agricultural advisors. In addition, disease-resistant varieties should be used where possible.

Invasiveness

Of the many factors to be considered when choosing trees, the danger of them spreading from the garden by seed and sucker to become invasive weeds is one of the most important. There are many well-documented cases of plants and animals becoming major pests in some areas. The European holly, *Ilex aquifolium,* thrives in the cool, moist conditions encountered in the northwestern states of the USA, and has spread into forests at the expense of the native vegetation. Government agricultural and environmental departments produce lists of potentially invasive species and these should be referred to before planting species that have the ability to spread.

Health and safety

Some trees have toxic leaves, fruit, or seeds, while others are armed with thorns. Where trees are being chosen for planting close to areas used by the public, and especially children, these factors should be borne in mind and will make certain species unsuitable.

Although highly desirable for their spectacular berries, most species and varieties of Sorbus *(left) are susceptible to fireblight.*

13

Finding and selecting trees

Having come up with a list of suitable trees, the job of finding suppliers and selecting the best individual plants can begin. Many of the more common species and cultivars will be relatively easy to find at general garden centers. Others will require a more specialized tree nursery and, where none is available in the area, the use of mail order. At one time this method of obtaining plants had a bad reputation, but with great improvements in packaging methods and rapid delivery times it has become a good way to obtain unusual plants. The Internet has further increased the potential for mail-order sales, making it possible to track down almost any plant in cultivation. In addition, many websites include photographs and a wealth of useful information about the size, cultural requirements, and tending of the plants in question. The only downside to mail ordering plants is that they can't be examined individually before purchase, and although rejection is possible it is time-consuming and inconvenient to return them.

Whatever source of plants is used, the selection process does not end with the species chosen. Plants may be available pot-grown or bare-rooted and in a variety of sizes. However, by far the most important factor is to select well-grown, healthy plants. It is almost invariably a mistake to buy sickly looking plants with the belief that they will "pull through" once planted—they rarely do.

Selecting healthy plants

Since the majority of plants offered for sale in modern garden centers are of a high standard, it would, perhaps, be better to describe this process as "rejection of unhealthy plants." Most of the signs to look out for are fairly obvious, while others require more careful scrutiny.

- Quality-grown plants have a general look of well-being, with labels that clearly identify what they are
- Leaves are a good indicator of plant health and should be appropriately colored (usually green) without signs of insect damage
- Particular attention should be paid to the undersides of leaves where pests such as scale insects and aphids often lurk
- Undersized or yellowed leaves are an obvious sign of poor health, as is premature leaf loss
- Container-grown plants should be in appropriately sized pots and well watered
- Large plants left too long in a small container may be pot-bound, a condition that may prevent root spread once planted out. A mass of roots projecting from the drainage holes at the bottom of a pot is another indicator of this
- A dense cover of weeds on the surface of the compost is a sure sign that the plant has been in the container for some time
- A plant in too large a container may have been recently potted-on and be difficult to transplant without root disturbance
- Growth is an essential requirement for good plant health and extension of terminal shoots can provide a good indicator. Regular and clear spacing between successive years' growth nodes is usually easy to see and a sure sign of a vigorous plant
- Check stems and branches for abrasions or breakages. Minor damage to twigs can be easily remedied by pruning, but injuries to the bark on main stems can allow disease entry and decay
- Plants with acutely forking main stems or no clear central leading shoot (where desirable) should also be rejected

Although formative pruning and training can, to some extent, guide a tree to the desired shape, there is no substitute for obtaining plants that are already showing a tendency to good form. Particular care should be taken when selecting larger plants over about 6 ft. (2m) in height. It is essential that the size of their root balls or containers are in proportion to their crowns if they are to survive transplanting. In addition, the main stem should show gradual taper from the ground to the base of the crown. Over-supportive staking from a young age can lead to a thin, untapered, stem that will later prove insufficiently strong to stand up to the stresses put upon it (see "Planting trees," page 16).

Bare-rooted or container-grown?

Bare-rooted trees are those that are grown in the open ground and dug up shortly before sale. Roots are delicate, very susceptible to both physical damage and drying out and, to be successful, bare-rooted trees need expert handing and packaging. For this reason it is unusual to see the use of truly bare-rooted trees for domestic purposes.

Far more common are so-called "root-balled" trees. Like bare-rooted trees, these are grown in open ground but after being dug up, the roots, along with a certain amount of the surrounding soil, are "balled" in various kinds of natural or synthetic burlap for protection. Although they may be kept in this state for some time during the dormant season, care must be taken to ensure roots are not exposed to frost or heat and are kept moist. Root-balling is particularly common on larger "standard" trees where growth to a sufficient size in a container would be difficult.

Most plants bought for general garden use are container-grown. Their great advantage is the ability to be transplanted from container to soil with minimal root disturbance. As well as suffering little set-back, this makes it possible, with some care, to plant them at any time of year. In addition, plants can be bought long before they are to be planted and kept in their containers until needed. The only real disadvantage of container-grown plants is an occasional reluctance for their roots to spread from the comfort of their original growing medium into the

It is always important to select a tree that is the right size for its intended location. Nyssa sinensis *(above) is a better choice for a small garden than its larger relative* N. sylvatica.

surrounding soil. This is most often a problem in poor or compacted soils, a situation that can be improved to some extent during planting.

Size

It is important to select plants of a suitable size. Large "standard" plants may promise quick results but often grow very slowly (if at all) after planting until their root systems catch up with their large crowns. In addition, they require careful staking or guying to prevent them blowing over. Very small plants, on the other hand, though cheaper, may be more susceptible to frost damage and swamping by surrounding vegetation.

In general, it is best to choose intermediate-sized plants, small enough not to require staking and with a good ratio of roots to crown. Some species such as *Nyssa sinensis* become increasingly difficult to transplant successfully with age and should only be bought when young.

Names and labeling

Plant classification is a complicated and contentious subject, a fact reflected in the frequent confusion over tree names. Commercial horticulture is often slow in responding to name changes, and those shown on labels do not always correspond exactly with the botanical ones given in books. Care should always be taken where ambiguity exists to check that the plant is what you think it is.

The beauty of attractive features like ornamental bark can be emphasized by careful positioning of trees in front of an evergreen background, and group planting.

Planting trees

As long as a few simple rules are followed, planting trees is not a difficult or complicated job. Of equal importance to how to plant is where to plant—and, more particularly, where not to plant.

Where to plant

The complexity of plant arrangement and garden design is too big a subject for this book but there are some simple considerations that should be borne in mind before positioning trees. Individual small trees rarely have a sufficiently striking presence to stand alone as strong specimens in their own right. More often they work to complement each other and soften the outlines of man-made features such as buildings and paths. They have great potential for screening unsightly objects, but care should be taken when positioning them to ensure that they will not block attractive views or fill valuable open space in the garden.

From a practical point of view, there are other factors to think about when planting in confined spaces and close to houses:

- The tree's ultimate size and how that will impact on its surroundings. A tree planted too close to a house can give a cramped and claustrophobic feel as well as shading the windows from welcome sunlight
- Remember that roots can cause damage to water pipes
- Fallen leaves may block drains and gutters
- The efficiency with which trees extract water from the soil is of particular importance. Roots spread far more widely than is commonly supposed; even moderately sized trees can have a marked effect on a surrounding lawn. On soils with a high clay content this drying frequently leads to shrinkage and the risk of subsidence to house foundations or driveways

This last point is a complex subject and there are no hard-and-fast rules about safe planting distances for trees from houses. Advice needs to be site-specific and where subsidence risk exists, advice should be sought from a qualified arboricultural advisor, (see resources, page 172).

One possibility often overlooked by small garden owners is that of planting trees in containers. As well as providing the opportunity to grow species unsuited to the local soil conditions, container growing may allow the cultivation of trees in very confined spaces where they would become too large if planting in the open ground. The only real downside to container plants is the extra attention needed. They must be regarded as pets requiring regular feeding and watering and a friendly neighbor if left for long during dry spells.

How to plant

Even before planting a tree, care must be taken to ensure that its roots are not allowed to dry out. Root-balled plants are particularly susceptible and should be kept in shade and watered until planting. The amount of ground preparation required is dependent on the condition of the soil.

1 *Remove any existing vegetation, particularly turf that may compete with the young tree.*

2 *On a well-drained moist soil very little more is needed and the hole should only be dug a little larger than required to accommodate the root spread of the plant.*

3 *In less amenable soils a larger hole at least twice the width and depth of the roots should be dug to improve the conditions in the area surrounding the young plant's roots.*

4 *On wet soils, sand or grit may be mixed with the backfill to improve drainage.*

5 *On rocky or compacted sites it is well worth loosening the soil for a distance around the roots to aid penetration.*

6 *On freely draining sandy sites, organic material such as rotted compost or leaf mold may be added to improve water and nutrient retention.*

Although these measures help to give young plants a good start, they have only a very localized effect and should not be regarded as sufficient to allow the planting of species unsuited to the prevailing soil type.

The transfer from pot or root-ball to soil is a critical time for a plant and it should be made as quick and stress-free as possible. Plants should be liberally watered before planting and left to stand for a while to give the compost time to soak. Container-grown plants should be carefully removed from their pots so as not to disturb the roots. They can then be placed into the dug hole and the gap around filled with soil and firmed.

Bare-rooted or burlapped plants should have all covering removed and the roots spread out in the hole. Care should be taken when firming the backfilled soil to avoid damage to the vulnerable roots.

Whatever kind of plants are used it is very important that the final soil level at the base of the stem is the same as the original. This is usually easy to judge by the presence of a distinct line marking the junction of root and stem known as the "nursery mark."

Where staking is necessary for stability, it should be driven into the base of the hole before planting. The tree can then be positioned alongside and tied loosely with a tree-tie after backfilling. On large container-grown plants where staking in this way would damage the roots, double staking with a crossbar is better.

Whichever method is used, it is very important in order to promote a strong stem that the tie is attached low down (less than one-third tree height) to allow plenty of flex. In addition, the tie must have a spacer to hold the stem clear of the stake to avoid bark rubbing.

When to plant

In general the best time to plant trees is during the dormant season. Container-grown plants may be planted at any time provided they are watered well. Evergreens are more liable to water loss when dormant than deciduous species and should, ideally, be planted in late fall or early spring when their roots are active and able to take up water.

Aftercare

Watering

By far the most important requirement for young trees is sufficient water. The first watering should be done directly after planting to drench the surrounding soil and help close any air pockets left after firming. Close attention should be paid to young trees during the first 2 or 3 growing seasons, especially during dry weather and on freely draining soils. When watering is necessary, it should be thorough to ensure penetration to the deeper roots. Once established, trees rarely need watering except in extreme conditions.

Weed control

Weed competition is a common cause of drought stress to young trees even in relatively moist soils and is a particular problem on lawns. To reduce surface moisture loss and reduce the need for watering a circle of at least 3 ft. (1m) diameter should be kept weed free by application of a mulch. This may be a layer of organic material such as shredded bark or leaf mold, or a porous synthetic textile made for the purpose. The latter is particularly effective where weed growth is strong and can be covered with organic material for the sake of appearance. Care should be taken to ensure when laying fabric that plenty of room is left around the stem to allow for growth. Organic mulches should be applied to a depth of at least 2 in. (5cm), leaving a gap of 4 in. (10cm) around the base of the stem to avoid the risk of pest damage. They have the additional benefits over textile mulches of helping to improve soil fertility and reducing compaction where human traffic is a problem.

Fertilizing

Providing suitable trees have been chosen for a particular site, fertilizing is rarely necessary apart from an occasional reapplication of organic mulch to maintain soil fertility. Container plants are the exception, requiring feeding with a slow-release general fertilizer during the growing season.

Maintenance of stakes

Poorly applied and maintained stakes are one of the most common causes of damage to young trees. Stakes should be removed as soon as the roots have developed enough to anchor the tree unaided. The time taken for this depends on the size and level of exposure of the tree, with those in windy positions requiring support for much longer than sheltered plants. In the meantime stakes and ties should be regularly inspected to ensure that there is no abrasion and the tie is kept loose.

Pruning

The main purpose of pruning ornamental trees is to create a specimen with a sound structure and attractive shape. In addition, it may be carried out to control the spread of disease or promote flowering or attractive foliage.

In general, garden trees require far less pruning than flowering shrubs and more damage is done by over-zealous "trimmers" than those who leave well alone. Drastic pruning to reduce the size of an overgrown tree is usually a sign of poor species choice and should be avoided if at all possible. Most trees have what may be regarded as their ideal shape and in a perfect world all individuals would attain it without the need for pruning.

The basics

The most important rule is to start any necessary pruning when the tree is young. As well as "nipping problems in the bud" early pruning has the advantage of leaving small wounds that heal quickly and run less risk of disease entry. Pruning cuts should be carefully positioned to do the least possible damage, and branches should be initially lightened to reduce the risk of bark tearing.

The best time of year to prune trees varies from one species to another. Most deciduous species may be pruned in winter or summer, avoiding the period around leaf emergence in spring and senescence in fall. Evergreen species, particularly less hardy ones, should be pruned after the danger of spring frosts has passed. A few species have very specific pruning times. Cherries, for example, should be pruned in mid-summer when they are least likely to become infected by silver-leaf or blossom wilt.

Pruning is greatly aided by the use of good-quality tools. Secateurs are suitable for branches up to about ½ in. (1.25cm). Loppers can be used on larger limbs up to about twice this size, above which pruning saws are best.

The strongest leader should be selected and favored by pruning its competitors back to the main stem.

Vigorous lower shoots should be shortened by pruning back to well below the selected leader.

Upper crown (above half height): Prune only dead or crossing branches back to the main stem.

Middle crown (below half height, above the lower crown): Prune lateral branches by about half their length.

Lower crown (bottom quarter): Prune out lateral branches back to the main stem.

As the young tree grows, continue to remove dead, damaged, or competing branches in the upper crown.

Extend the middle crown by shortening lateral branches up to new half height.

Prune out previously shortened lateral branches now in the lower crown back to the main stem.

Continue to prune out dead and crossing branches in the upper crown.

Prune out remaining shortened lateral branches to produce a clean stem.

Pruning to promote a dominant leader

Early removal of the weaker of two co-dominant stems will encourage a more upright shape and reduce the risk of developing a weak fork.

Pruning to produce a clear trunk

Where the aim is to produce a clean trunk, phased pruning can progressively remove branches from the bottom upward.

Pruning to remove reversion (right)

Sometimes cultivars selected for their unusual characteristics have a tendency to "revert" by producing branches or foliage with a more normal form. Weeping trees are a good example as are some of the variegated cultivars. Where reversion occurs, the offending branches should be quickly pruned out to discourage the tendency.

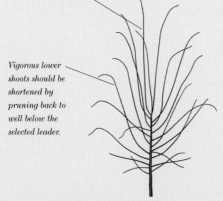

Pruning for disease

The spread of some diseases can be controlled by removing infected branches. Fireblight is a good example where, if caught early, infected areas can be pruned back to healthy wood and the prunings burnt. Tools should be sterilized between cuts to prevent disease spread.

Pruning to remove crossing branches and dead wood

Rubbing branches results in bark damage that can become a source of decay or disease entry. They should be pruned back to a side branch to avoid leaving stubs. Dead wood can be removed in a similar way for aesthetic reasons.

Directory of trees

The following directory of small trees is arranged alphabetically. As well as the 80 main trees, it includes related or similar supplementary trees to provide additional choice. Each plant is described with emphasis on the particular attributes that make it worth consideration for the small garden. The Factfinder with each description can be used as a quick check on size or cultural requirements.

Acer davidii
Père David's maple

Aceraceae

factfinder	
height	up to about 33 ft. (10m)
hardiness	zone 5
aspect	partial shade (best) to full sun
soil type	fertile, well drained
soil pH	acid to moderately alkaline
country of origin	central China

Acer davidii 'Ernest Wilson' (above) has small dark green leaves that usually lack the lobes seen on some other forms of the species. Mature trees produce abundant strings of small winged fruits.

The glossy green, patterned bark of this small Chinese tree marks it out as one of the group known as the "snake-bark" maples. Its other notable feature is its shining leaves that turn to orange and yellow in the fall and are often accompanied by equally colorful winged fruits. It is variable in both height and shape but typically grows to about 33 ft. (10m) with a broad and open crown. It may be single or multiple-stemmed, the latter giving greater scope for display of its attractive bark. This benefits from an occasional stroke to clean off dirt and algae and maintain its beautiful sheen.

Although it grows well on a variety of soil types, it does best on a deep, well-drained loam, ranging from acid to moderately alkaline. It is a hardy tree, but is best grown in a sheltered location in dappled shade.

Other trees

The form most often seen in cultivation is 'George Forrest.' It has an open habit and leaves that turn orange and red in fall. The less common 'Ernest Wilson' has a more compact shape and is considered to display superior fall leaf color. 'Serpentine' is a cultivar grown for its particularly ornamental bark.

The closely related tree often known as *Acer grosseri* is now considered to be a subspecies of *A. davidii*. Its gray-green bark is particularly striking with a fine patterning of white veins. It is also known as *A. grosseri* var. *hersii* or *A. hersii*, though some authorities consider these to be a separate and distinct form of the species.

The bark of cultivar 'Serpentine' is strongly striped with white, and looks particularly striking on multiple-stemmed trees.

Like many maples, the pale yellow flowers (left) have a delicate beauty that deserves close examination. They are arranged in pendulous racemes about 3 in. (8cm) long.

Acer davidii ssp. grosseri (right) is a commonly seen and easily obtained form of the species. Fine specimens like this are often multiple stemmed with low sweeping branches.

The blunt-toothed leaves are dark green above with paler hairy undersides. They are composed of 3 leaflets that color attractively in fall. The fruits have broad yellow-green wings.

Acer griseum
Paper-bark maple

Aceraceae

With its attractive peeling bark and superb fall color, this is undoubtedly one of the most beautiful and recognizable of all the maples. It is a native of China but has become a firm favorite in North America and Europe. Although its neat, compact shape makes it ideal for gardens, on a favorable site it can reach a height of about 40 ft. (12m) with a similar spread, and it is therefore not suitable for those of very small size. The flowers, though inconspicuous, give rise to attractive winged "helicopter" fruits typical of the genus, and in fall the "un-maple-like" leaves turn an array of bright colors through red and orange. It makes a wonderful specimen that demands pride of place on a lawn or open border.

It is an easy tree to grow, being well suited to cool climates and requiring no special pruning or other tending. It will tolerate most well-drained soils, both acid and alkaline, but grows poorly on shallow soils over chalk. Even fairly large standard saplings can be transplanted successfully, though smaller plants are best, and it is widely available from non-specialist plant centers and nurseries. It may also be raised from seed, but the rate of viability is usually very low.

Other trees

Unlike many other species of maple, *Acer griseum* has no wild or cultivated varieties. However, for those wanting something similar but unusual, the less common *Acer triflorum* is a somewhat smaller relative of this species with vertically peeling gray-brown bark. It too displays excellent fall color and is obtainable from more specialized nurseries or by special order.

The new leaves and flowers of Acer triflorum *(left) appear at about the same time, the latter arranged in groups of three.*

The closely related species Acer triflorum *(above right) has a similar shape to* A. griseum *and provides an interesting alternative for those seeking something different.*

factfinder

height	up to about 40 ft. (12m)
hardiness	zone 4
aspect	full sun to partial shade
soil type	moist, well drained
soil pH	lime free
country of origin	central China

The bark is rusty red in color and peels in thin flakes even on young trees.

Grown as a lawn specimen (right), Paper-bark maple's combination of attractive features provides all-year-round interest as well as a strong visual focus.

Acer japonicum
Full moon maple

Aceraceae

The leaves of 'Vitifolium' (above) are a little larger than those of the species. They tend to color earlier than other forms and provide a spectacular and long-lived show of intense red.

Although similar in many ways to Japanese maple, *Acer palmatum,* this close relative can be distinguished by its rounded, less deeply lobed leaves. It usually reaches the stature of a small tree, and when given sufficient space can spread outward with long horizontal branches, sometimes supported by the ground. Its small flowers appear in spring at about the same time as the leaves and, although often overlooked, have a delicate beauty typical of maples. The flowers are followed by fruits that hang in pairs, made conspicuous by their red-tinged green wings. However, this tree's main attraction lies in its leaves, that turn to glorious shades of red and orange in the fall.

Although hardy, this tree is best grown in a sheltered position away from cold winds. It is particularly suitable as an understorey plant in the partial shade of larger trees and prefers a moist, well-drained soil.

A. japonicum usually develops with a number of limbs forming a broad spreading tree (right).

factfinder

height	up to about 33 ft. (10m)
hardiness	zone 5
aspect	partial shade (best) or full sun
soil type	moist, well drained
soil pH	acid to neutral
country of origin	Japan

The leaves (below) are rounded with 7 to 11 toothed lobes and give the tree its common name. Acer japonicum (right) is often one of the earliest maples to color in fall, providing contrast with the later coloring Acer palmatum and its cultivars.

Other trees

Despite its popularity and long history of cultivation, full moon maple has given rise to far fewer cultivars than *A. palmatum.* However, two are of particular note. The leaves of 'Vitifolium' have a similar shape to the species, but color to a deep red in the fall. Those of 'Aconitifolium' are deeply cut down to the base into narrow, toothed lobes. Both have a similar stature to the species. *A. shirasawanum* is a closely related species best known for the cultivar 'Aureum,' a slow-growing form with brilliant golden-green leaves.

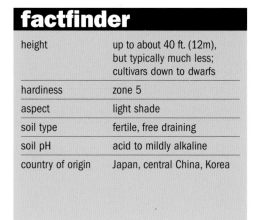

Acer palmatum
Japanese maple

Aceraceae

The leaves of 'Katsura' (above) are deeply divided and renowned for their spring color, gradually changing from pale yellow-green to orange. 'Ozakazuki' (below) is one of the best known cultivars.

One of the most versatile trees for almost any garden, Japanese maple exists in a multitude of forms that provide an almost endless choice of sizes, colors, and shapes. Its 5- or 7-lobed palmate (hand-shaped) leaves are its main feature, particularly in the fall when they turn a dazzling array of colors. It varies in size from large shrub to small tree with a broadly spreading crown, and is frequently multiple stemmed. The main trunks often grow in sinuous curves that provide visual appeal even during the leafless months of winter. Although most often seen as grafted cultivars, the species itself has much to commend it, being less expensive and more tolerant of adverse climates. On the downside, seed-grown plants are less predictable in size and leaf coloration than named selections.

The cultivars vary greatly in their requirements for shade and shelter depending largely on their leaf shape and color. In general, the finely divided 'Dissectum' forms are the most delicate and require protection from exposure and direct sunlight. The red and more robustly leaved forms can be grown in full sunlight; many will not develop their full color in heavy shade.

All types require a fertile, well-drained soil, and although tolerant of mildly alkaline conditions,

factfinder

height	up to about 40 ft. (12m), but typically much less; cultivars down to dwarfs
hardiness	zone 5
aspect	light shade
soil type	fertile, free draining
soil pH	acid to mildly alkaline
country of origin	Japan, central China, Korea

will not give their best. Where space or soil conditions dictate, the smaller cultivars can all be grown in containers and provide an excellent alternative to ground plants.

Other trees

The cultivation and selective breeding of Japanese maple goes back over three centuries. Characteristics such as leaf shape, growth form, and seasonal coloration have all been carefully selected to produce a vast range of cultivars. There are now more than 300 to choose from, varying in size from that of the species down to dwarfs. Some have been selected for the brilliance of their spring leaves, while others display attractively colored bark. For a comprehensive list of cultivars, readers should refer to one of the specialist books on the subject.

Forms with finely divided green leaves such as 'Dissectum' (far left) benefit from partial shade to protect their foliage. 'Crimson Queen' (left) has red dissected leaves and is suitable for growing in full sun. It forms a mound up to about 12 ft. (3.6m).

Among the most ornamental forms of A. palmatum are the dissected-leaved cultivars, including 'Dissectum' (above). It grows slowly to a height of little over 6 ft. (2m) and forms a fountain of finely divided foliage that turns fiery orange in fall.

Even in its species form (left), the foliage of A. palmatum provides a delicate beauty perfect for the small garden.

29

'Deshojo' (above and bottom right) is one of the most striking cultivars for spring color. Its new leaves are brilliant carmine pink, soon fading to a quieter shade of pale green. It grows to about 12ft. (3.6m).

Although best known for its colored shoots, 'Senkaki' also puts on an impressive display of yellow-orange fall color.

The variety of foliage is almost endless. The leaves of 'Shishigashira' (above left) are curly and bunched and turn orange and crimson in fall.

'Sango kaku' (above right) is also known as 'coral-bark maple' due to its brightly colored shoots.

The fruits (above) are held in pairs and hang in long-stalked clusters. They are made conspicuous by their red wings.

Acer pseudoplatanus 'Brilliantissimum'
Sycamore (cultivar)
Aceraceae

The new leaves are glossy and unfurl gradually. As they mature they pass through various shades of pink and bronze to yellow-green.

The European sycamore is a large tree suitable only for big gardens and parks. However, this cultivar of the species is more modestly sized and is one of the most spectacular small trees for spring color. Its lobed leaves open a vibrant shade of pink and gradually fade through yellow to pale green as the season progresses. It grows slowly into a compact, single-stemmed tree with a neat rounded crown, making it a great choice for small avenues or other semi-formal situations. It is very tolerant of a wide variety of soil types and may be grown in full sun or partial shade.

The yellow flowers (above) hang in dense clusters at the same time as the new leaves.

Other trees

Where space allows, another striking sycamore cultivar suitable for larger gardens is the golden sycamore (*A. pseudoplatanus* 'Worleei'). During spring this medium-sized tree has yellow leaves that change to golden and eventually green.

Note: Sycamore regularly produces large quantities of viable seed and has the potential to be invasive. It should not be cultivated close to areas where it may colonize native vegetation.

factfinder

height	up to about 33 ft. (10m); 'Worleei' 50–65 ft. (15–20m)
hardiness	zone 4
aspect	full sun to partial shade
soil type	any fertile
soil pH	very tolerant
country of origin	Europe, western Asia (species)
observation	potentially invasive

Set against a background of dark-foliaged plants, even small trees (left) create a strong visual focus.

31

Aesculus × neglecta 'Erythroblastos'
Sunrise horse chestnut

Hippocastanaceae

The leaves (above) have the typical 5-fingered shape of horse chestnuts. When newly emerged, they are among the most brilliant of all spring coloring trees.

This is one of the very best small trees for spring leaf color. It is a cultivated form of a natural hybrid between the two North American species *A. flava* and *A. sylvatica*. The original tree grew in Berlin in about the 1930s, since when it has given rise to plants all over the world. It grows slowly to a height that seldom exceeds 26 ft. (8m) and has a rounded or columnar crown. The emergent leaves are a brilliant salmon pink with 5 narrow, partially opened leaflets. They gradually fade to pale green by late spring when they may be joined by the rather unreliable pale yellow flowers. In some years the turning leaves display good fall colors of orange and yellow.

In common with most buckeyes it is tolerant of alkaline soils but thrives best in those of a slightly acid pH. It is best grown in partial shade and looks particularly good with a dark evergreen background to emphasize the color of its new leaves. Although a very seasonal tree, its spring display is quite memorable and for the rest of the year it is quite content to grow in a confined space among other more dominant trees.

factfinder

height	up to about 26 ft. (8m)
hardiness	zone 5
aspect	partial shade
soil type	fertile, free draining
soil pH	very tolerant
country of origin	southeastern USA (hybrid)
observation	slow growing

Once fully opened (above) the leaves fade through yellow to pale green in early summer (left). At its peak of color, a mature specimen (right) becomes a strong focus of attention and provides a novel seasonal feature.

The flowers of A. pavia 'Atrosanguinea' are deep crimson, slightly darker than the species, held in upright panicles in early to mid-summer. The leaves are composed of 5 toothed leaflets, and turn red in fall.

Aesculus pavia
Red buckeye

Hippocastanaceae

Many buckeyes (horse chestnuts) are too large for most gardens. This species rarely exceeds 20 ft. (6m) in height and provides an unusual option for restricted spaces. It varies in shape from a spreading shrub-like plant to a rounded tree with a dense crown. The flowers are bright crimson and appear in early to mid-summer. They give rise to small, pear-shaped fruits that enclose a single or pair of glossy seeds or "buckeyes." Although tolerant of a wide range of soils, buckeye does not thrive in dry or exposed conditions. Its ability to grow in shade makes it suitable for gardens that lack full sunlight.

Like those of many buckeyes, the leaves of A. pavia color early and are accompanied by pear-like fruit.

Other trees

The best-known cultivar is 'Atrosanguinea,' a form varying only in its rather darker flowers. Ohio buckeye, *A. glabra*, is another small American species that produces its yellow flowers from a young age. They are borne in late spring and are followed by spined fruits. In addition, the leaves often color yellow and orange in the fall.

When given sufficient space, A. pavia (left) often forms a spreading multiple-stemmed tree. This results in low foliage and flowers.

factfinder

height	up to about 20 ft. (6m); *A. glabra* 33 ft. (10m)
hardiness	zone 4 (*A. glabra* 7)
aspect	full sun to partial shade
soil type	moist, free draining
soil pH	very tolerant
country of origin	southern USA

The leaves (above) are up to 4 in. (10cm) long, with irregular teeth and slightly lobed edges.

Alnus incana 'Aurea'
European gray alder
(cultivar)

Betulaceae

In its native Europe this species is often seen growing along river banks with its roots partly in the water. Its ability to grow in waterlogged soils and fix atmospheric nitrogen makes it invaluable for planting in poorly drained and nutrient-deficient conditions where few other species will grow.

However, it is a strongly growing tree that can reach a height of well over 65 ft. (20m), and is therefore too large for most gardens. The cultivar 'Aurea' is much smaller, rarely exceeding 40 ft. (12m) with a broadly conical shape. Its most notable feature is its golden foliage, particularly conspicuous when the leaves are young. Like the species, it also provides interest in winter and early spring when the male catkins hang exposed from bare branches. The smaller female catkins ripen into dried "cones" and persist on the tree long after the tiny seeds have been shed. In the garden, its most obvious application is as a pond-side tree but its strong outline and attractive foliage make it suitable for a range of situations, either as an individual specimen or in a small group.

The bark is gray and remains smooth, even in older trees.

The foliage (right) has a yellow tinge, particularly when young. In late summer the tone is less pronounced, but leaves acquire a green/yellow variegation. The male catkins are orange, and hang from the shoot ends in great abundance from fall through winter.

A. incana 'Aurea' develops a neat conical shape and contrasts well with a dark background of evergreens.

factfinder

height	about 40 ft. (12m)
hardiness	zone 2 (A. glutinosa 3)
aspect	full sun
soil type	very tolerant
soil pH	very tolerant
country of origin	Europe, Caucasus

Other trees

'Laciniata' is a form with dissected leaves while 'Pendula' makes a small weeping tree with gray-green leaves. European alder, *A. glutinosa*, is a species with a number of cultivars suitable for gardens. 'Imperialis' has leaves that are cut into narrow lobes giving them a delicate, feather-like appearance. 'Pyramidalis' ('Fastigiata') is a narrowly columnar form suitable for screening or use as a windbreak.

The star-shaped flowers are borne in upright racemes and have 5 narrow petals. They are often accompanied by the emerging leaves that start a beautiful shade of bronze, later becoming dark green and fine toothed.

The Dutch cultivar A. 'Ballerina' (below) is popular for its vigorous growth and abundant flowers. It often forms a spreading tree with low branches almost at ground level.

Amelanchier lamarckii
Snowy mespilus, serviceberry

Rosaceae

Amelanchier is a small genus of trees and shrubs grown primarily for their delicate white spring flowers and fine fall leaf color. This species is one of the best, being easy to obtain and grow. It is often seen as a multi-stemmed shrub but can develop into a small tree with a broadly spreading shape. Its star-like flowers appear in early spring at about the same time as the opening leaves and, although short-lived, provide a dazzling display that is long remembered. The flowers are followed by small sweet-tasting black fruits that ripen by mid-summer. In common with other members of the genus, the leaves provide color both in the spring when newly open and again in the fall.

This is a very hardy species that requires a lime-free, well-drained soil. It does not thrive in very dry conditions and young plants in particular benefit from watering during dry spells. It is best grown in an open location where it can grow and flower freely. Fireblight may be a problem in some areas.

factfinder

height	up to about 40 ft. (12m)
hardiness	zone 4
aspect	full sun (best) to partial shade
soil type	moist, free draining
soil pH	lime free
country of origin	eastern North America
observation	may be affected by fireblight

Other trees

There are about 10 species of *Amelanchier* in cultivation. The other frequently seen species is the North American *A. laevis*. It is thought to be a parent of the popular hybrid cultivar *A.* 'Ballerina,' a Dutch selection that produces an abundant show of large white flowers and excellent fall color. *A. lamarckii* is often grown under the name *A. canadensis*, a similar but separate and less common species. *A. arborea* is another American species whose berries make a popular dessert.

The display of fall foliage (above) can be dramatic, with red and orange the dominant colors.

An extremely versatile tree, Amelachier lamarckii *can look as good in a highly designed urban setting (above) as is does in less formal situations. Careful formative pruning can create an interesting shape even with multiple-stemmed plants.*

The American species A. arborea *(left) is a popular choice in gardens of northeastern USA. As well as being an abundant flowerer, it has a reputation for fine fall color.*

Aralia elata
Japanese angelica tree
Araliaceae

The enormous compound leaves of this impressive plant sometimes measure 4 ft. (1.2m) in length and give it an unusual fern-like appearance. They arise in clusters from the ends of thick, often spined, stems that some regard as ugly and hide behind low-growing shrubs. The late summer/early fall flowers consist of frothy white panicles and are on a similar scale to the leaves. They may be accompanied by the color of early-turning leaves. Although usually a fairly upright small tree, many plants have a tendency to produce suckers that can, if left unpruned, develop into a thick clump. They may be lifted when still young and successfully transplanted.

Despite its ease of cultivation and novel appearance, this is a plant that is rarely seen in gardens. It may be grown in full sun or partial shade and will succeed in most free-draining soils. The large leaves are vulnerable to strong winds and a measure of shelter is desirable.

The remarkable leaves are among the largest of all hardy trees. They are double pinnate with leaflets further divided into secondary leaflets making one huge leaf up to 4 ft. (1.2m) long. In fall they turn to shades of orange and red.

The bark is covered in fine spines that, although an interesting feature, need considering when the species is planted in public areas.

Other trees

There are two well-known cultivars of the species, both with variegated leaves. *A. elata* 'Variegata' has leaflets with creamy-white margins, while those of 'Aureomarginata' are yellow-margined early in the year, gradually turning to white.

A. spinosa originates in southeastern USA and is a close relative of *A. elata*. It is very similar in most respects but flowers earlier in the year from mid-summer.

From late summer to early fall the large panicles of white flowers appear, sometimes coinciding with the first signs of fall color.

factfinder

height	up to about 33 ft. (10m)
hardiness	zone 4
aspect	full sun to partial shade
soil type	fertile, free draining
soil pH	moderately acid or alkaline
country of origin	Japan
observation	requires shelter from strong winds

Aralia elata is an adaptable tree, able to grow in full sunshine or the partial shade of other trees (right). Its late flowering can be of great value in the garden at a time of year when little else is in bloom.

Arbutus unedo
Killarney strawberry tree
Ericaceae

The combination of evergreen habit and tolerance of lime soils makes this a valuable plant for many garden situations. Although frequently more of a shrub than a tree, it can grow up to about 33 ft. (10m) in a suitable location with a broadly spreading shape. Unusually it produces its small, urn-shaped white flowers and larger red fruits at about the same time in the fall, the latter arising from the previous year's flowers. The leaves have a glossy sheen that contrasts with the roughly textured deep brown bark.

Although tolerant of a wide range of soil types and pH, it thrives best on a fertile and well-drained soil. It can withstand a high degree of wind exposure but is not suitable for areas where this is combined with very low temperatures. It is primarily a Mediterranean plant that prefers full sunlight to encourage good growth and flower production.

The beautiful bark of A. x andrachnoides *extends beyond the main trunk into the branches.*

Other trees

There are several other species of *Arbutus* in cultivation. *A.* x *andrachnoides* is a hybrid between *A. unedo* and the more tender Greek strawberry tree, *A. andrachne*. It has a similar stature to *A. unedo*, with conspicuous orange-red peeling bark. The North American *A. menziesii* also has attractive red bark but is much too large for most gardens, reaching up to 130 ft. (40m) in height.

Two cultivars of *A. unedo* are particularly worthy of note. Where space is at a premium, 'Elfin King' makes a medium-sized shrub of about 6 ft. (2m) in height and similar spread. 'Rubra' is a full-sized variety but varies in having pink flowers and a greater abundance of fruits.

The white flowers (above) are urn-shaped and born in nodding clusters in the fall. The evergreen leaves are glossy green above with fine teeth.

The flowers of A. unedo *'Rubra' (right) are pink. Like the species, they are borne at the same time as the strawberry-like fruits that arise from the previous year's flowers and give the tree its name.* A. unedo *(far right) forms a densely foliaged tree, ideal for many situations where evergreen habit and wide soil tolerance is needed.*

factfinder	
height	up to about 33 ft. (10m); some cultivars smaller
hardiness	zone 7 (*A. x andrachnoides* 8)
aspect	full sun (best) to partial shade
soil type	fertile, well drained
soil pH	very tolerant
country of origin	Mediterranean region, Ireland

Azara microphylla
Box-leaf azara

Flacourtiaceae

The leaves (above) are small and glossy, each with an accompanying stipule close to its base. The tiny yellow flowers are held in the leaf axils.

This beautiful evergreen deserves to be planted more widely than it is. Its name refers to its tiny leaves, arranged in an orderly fashion along the branches to create large fan-like sprays. The flowers, though small, are numerous enough to produce an overall haze of color and give off a scent of vanilla. It varies in stature from a large multi-stemmed shrub to a small tree with a fairly narrow upright shape. Although one of the hardiest species of Azara, it benefits from shelter in all but the mildest areas and does particularly well when grown against a wall. It will grow on most fertile, well-drained soils.

This is a fairly unusual plant that is not obtainable from all plant centers and nurseries. However, for those wanting something a bit different, it is well worth searching for. It is also worth considering for landscaping situations where the combination of delicate foliage and evergreen habit is desirable.

factfinder

height	up to about 33 ft. (10m), but typically much less
hardiness	zone 8
aspect	full sun to partial shade
soil type	fertile, well drained
soil pH	all but extremes
country of origin	Chile, Argentina
observation	requires sheltered site

Other trees

'Variegata' is the only commonly grown cultivar. It is slower growing than the species, with cream-margined leaves.

Several other species of *Azara* are in cultivation but only *A. serrata* is fairly readily available. Its serrated leaves are somewhat larger than those of *A. microphylla*, as are the orange flowers that appear in mid-summer.

The cultivar 'Variegata' (above and left) can be distinguished by its irregularly cream-margined leaves. Like the species, it is well suited to being grown in the protective shelter of a wall and may be trained to form an attractive screen of foliage.

The small branches and shoots (above) have purple-brown bark that becomes a feature in winter when illuminated by bright sunlight.

The smooth bark is pale gray or white with a pattern of horizontal lenticels. It is often broken up with raised patches of rougher bark that produce an interesting contrast.

The weeping foliage hangs right to the ground, providing opportunity for a range of visual effects in a designed garden.

Betula pendula 'Youngii'
Young's weeping birch

Betulaceae

The European silver birch, although a beautiful tree in its own right, is rather too large for most gardens. This cultivar combines the white bark and finely textured foliage of the species in a more compact form. It eventually forms a small tree up to about 33 ft. (10m) tall, its outstanding feature being the drooping branches that hang down to the ground and provide all-year-round interest. The effect is enhanced by catkins that arrive before the leaves in early spring. In some years the foliage provides good fall color, and in winter sunlight the leafless crown takes on a beautiful purple tinge.

It is a particularly hardy tree, able to survive extremely cold climates and exposure. It tolerates a wide range of soil types and pH, thriving even on poor sandy sites. The open crown casts a light shade making it an ideal tree for providing shelter and partial shade for less hardy species. It grows best in full sunlight.

Other trees

Silver birch has many other cultivars. One group, known as the cut-leaved birches, contains a number of forms grown for their attractively lacerated leaves. There is some inconsistency in their naming and, where eventual size is important, care should

The combination of graceful shape and white-patterned bark makes 'Youngii' a truly all-year-round tree. It is particularly effective planted in a group so that the weeping crowns merge into one.

be taken in selection. One of them, 'Gracilis,' grows to about 33 ft. (10m) tall and has deeply cut leaves. 'Laciniata,' although similar in leaf shape, grows into a full-sized specimen with a distinctly weeping habit. It is sometimes incorrectly named 'Dalecarlica,' a less common selection with a reduced weeping tendency.

factfinder

height	up to about 33 ft. (10m)
hardiness	zone 2
aspect	full sun
soil type	any
soil pH	very tolerant
country of origin	Europe

Betula utilis
Himalayan birch

Betulaceae

Best known for its strikingly colored bark, this is a highly desirable garden plant. It is firmly in the category of a medium-sized tree with the potential to reach a height of 65ft. (20m) or more with a broadly conical crown. Unfortunately it is often grown in spaces too small for its mature dimensions necessitating ugly crown reduction pruning. Luckily, it is adaptable enough to grow quite happily in large planters or restricted beds where it grows to a much more modest size, allowing it to be positioned for best visual effect. Its graceful branch and twig structure is a feature throughout the year, supplemented in the spring by long male catkins. The bark is highly variable in color, ranging from almost pure white through orange-brown and pink to deep copper. The effect is added to by the habit of peeling in strips to reveal contrastingly colored underlayers.

It is a very hardy plant that will tolerate a range of soil types and pH. However, in common with other birch species, it becomes susceptible to damage by insect borers and miners in particularly warm, dry conditions.

Other trees

The species' variability has resulted in a number of inconsistently named varieties and cultivars, differing mainly in their bark color. *B. utilis* var. *jacquemontii* (*B. jacquemontii*) is probably the best known for its brilliant white bark. It is most often seen as one of a number of named cultivars. 'Doorenbos' is a Dutch selection whose white bark peels to reveal orange underlayers. 'Silver Shadow' originates from the famous Hillier Nurseries in Hampshire, England, and is a little smaller than the variety and perhaps the most brilliantly white-barked of all the forms.

The ovate leaves (top) have glossy dark green upper surfaces and fine teeth, often turning bright yellow in fall. The pale patterned bark extends beyond the main trunk into the smaller branches of the crown (above).

The smooth peeling bark varies widely in color from almost pure white to copper (left), and is patterned with horizontal bands known as lenticels.

factfinder	
height	up to about 65 ft. (20m)
hardiness	zone 3
aspect	full sun
soil type	tolerant (but not suitable for very dry sites)
soil pH	acid or alkaline
country of origin	southwest China to Nepal
observation	unsuitable for hot, dry climates

Trees should be grown in an open position (above and right) where their trunks will not be obscured from view. They often look particularly effective grown in small groups against a dark background.

Cultivars and varieties vary primarily in their bark coloration. 'Silver Shadow' (above left) and var. jacquemontii (above right) both have very pale bark with subtle shades of gray or buff.

The needles are up to ¾ in. (2cm) long and are held close to the shoots in dense whorls.

Cedrus atlantica 'Glauca Pendula'
Weeping blue Atlas cedar

Pinaceae

Few people are lucky enough to have a garden big enough to grow a full-sized Atlas cedar. This cultivar makes a small graceful tree that, although very different, is an interesting alternative. When full grown, its pendulous branches and blue-gray needles hang to the ground to form a curtain of foliage. This is particularly effective when grown as a specimen, carefully positioned to provide contrast with other forms and colors.

Because shape is of the essence, selection of planting stock and cultivation is very important. Ideally, plants should be grafted high onto the rootstock to give a straight stem from which the weeping crown can cascade. The alternative is to train the grafted branches upward from a lower level to achieve a similar result eventually. Needless to say, the former is by far the easier method and is recommended for those in a hurry. If left untrained, a low-grafted plant will develop an almost prostrate form. Although preferring a well-drained moist soil, it tolerates a range of soil types and pH including clays and limestone.

The combination of blue-green foliage and strongly weeping habit makes this a very distinctive tree.

factfinder

height	up to about 33 ft. (10m) depending on height of graft and training
hardiness	zone 6
aspect	full sun to partial shade
soil type	tolerant
soil pH	tolerant
country of origin	northwest Africa (species)
observation	susceptible to honey fungus

Other trees

C. atlantica 'Pendula' shares the weeping shape of 'Glauca Pendula' but is distinguished by its gray-green rather than blue foliage. There are a number of cultivars of other species of cedar. Most are either full-sized specimens or spreading shrubs. Worth considering for small gardens is *C. deodara* 'Aurea,' a form of Deodar cedar whose foliage is golden in the spring, gradually turning green. It grows slowly to a height of about 16 ft. (5m).

Where trees are grafted low and left untrained (above) they develop a low, undulating form that combines well with contrastingly shaped plants. To get a more upright tree, training is required (left). A long pole is required up which a main stem can be tied progressively higher as it grows.

The leaves are rounded, often heart-shaped at the base and arranged alternately along the shoots. They often open bronze-colored, turning bright green.

Cercis canadensis
Eastern redbud, Judas tree

Leguminosae

Best known for its spectacular display of spring flowers, this native plant of eastern USA is an ideal garden tree. It rarely grows more than 33 ft. (10m) tall with a similar spread and an ornamental, rounded shape. The pea-like flowers develop before the leaves in spring, emerging in clusters along the shoots, branches, and even trunk. By mid-summer, they are replaced by long, bean-like seed pods that persist through the fall. The emergent leaves are a deep purple, gradually changing to green. In some years they also color yellow in the fall.

This is a relatively easy tree to grow, particularly suited to sunny situations and well-drained soils. It tolerates acid or alkaline soils but is not successful on wet sites. It has a reputation for being difficult to transplant and is best planted small and moved only when young during the dormant season. On unsuitable sites it may become susceptible to verticillium wilt (fungal disease).

The pea-like flowers (right) arise directly from old shoots and branches on short stalks. They appear in late spring before the emergence of the leaves.

C. canadensis (above) becomes a low-branching tree or large shrub. In the fall the leaves turn yellow.

factfinder

height	up to about 33ft. (10m)
hardiness	zone 4 (*C. siliquastrum* 6)
aspect	full sun
soil type	free draining
soil pH	acid to moderately alkaline
country of origin	southeast USA

Other trees

Of similar stature (but less abundant in flower) is the European Judas tree, *C. siliquastrum*. This is the species from which, legend has it, Judas Iscariot hanged himself. It is native to the Mediterranean region and is less hardy than *C. canadensis*. For garden use, two cultivars are of particular merit. *C. canadensis* 'Forest Pansy' is less abundant in flower than the species but is grown for its impressive leaves that retain their deep purple color through most of the growing season. It may be grown as a regularly cut stump from which new shoots arise with spectacular over-sized leaves. 'Alba' is a white-flowered cultivar, otherwise similar to the species.

One of the most popular cultivars is C. canadensis *'Forest Pansy' (left). Its leaves remain purple-bronze throughout summer and it is particularly effective when combined with dark-petalled flowers.*

The foliage of the cultivar 'Spiralis' (above) grows with a twisted habit. The male flowers are yellow and mass at the tips of the shoots. 'Spiralis Aurea' (below) has similar but golden foliage and, like 'Spiralis,' grows to about 3 ft. (1m).

Chamaecyparis obtusa
Hinoki cypress (cultivars)

Cupressaceae

In its wild form Hinoki cypress is a large tree grown for its timber. Luckily for gardeners, it has given rise to numerous garden cultivars, many originating in its native Japan. They vary greatly in size, from large trees to tiny dwarfs, and display a range of foliage that provides growers with almost endless choice. The slow-growing and dwarf varieties are suitable for rock gardens and, where local soil conditions are unhelpful, may be grown in containers with suitable compost. Readers should consult a specialist book to investigate the full range of available cultivars (see page 172). This is a hardy tree that is generally considered more suitable for colder, continental-type climates than its American relative *C. lawsoniana* and its cultivars.

factfinder

height	variable; dwarf to large tree
hardiness	zone 4
aspect	full sun to partial shade
soil type	fertile, free draining
soil pH	acid to moderately alkaline
country of origin	Japan (species)

Other trees

Of the tree forms, 'Crippsii' is a slow-growing selection that eventually develops a broad and irregular conical shape up to about 33 ft. (10m) tall. Its rich golden foliage is arranged on irregular, open branches that droop toward their tips, giving an elegant appearance. 'Nana Gracilis' is a popular form with unusual fern-like sprays of glossy green foliage. It develops into a dense shrub up to about 16 ft. (5m) in height with an amorphous shape that provides a wealth of design possibilities. 'Spiralis' is a dwarf bush that reaches only 3 ft. (1m) and has unusual twisted foliage. 'Nana Aurea' is an excellent selection that, though tree shaped, rarely exceeds 6 ft. (2m) in height with golden yellow foliage.

The foliage of 'Nana Aurea' (above) is arranged in flattened sprays. Its golden color is particularly conspicuous on new growth and in winter.

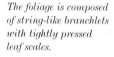

Chamaecyparis pisifera 'Filifera'
Sawara cypress (cultivar)

Cupressaceae

The foliage is composed of string-like branchlets with tightly pressed leaf scales.

For situations where a large mass of interesting foliage is wanted, this tree is ideal. Its breadth often exceeds its height of up to about 33ft. (10m) resulting in a broad, round-topped pyramid shape. The cultivar name is derived from its thread-like foliage that hangs from drooping branchlets and provides its unusual texture. Although not an obvious choice as a specimen plant, when carefully positioned in the garden it can act as a valuable complement to other contrastingly colored and textured plants. It may also be used for screening where a combination of function and visual interest is needed.

Other trees

'Filifera Aurea' is similar, but with golden foliage that tends to emphasize its texture. Numerous other cultivars of the species are available providing a huge choice of size, color, and texture. For larger gardens 'Squarrosa,' with its soft gray feathery foliage, is particularly attractive.

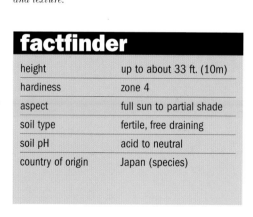

'Filifera' (above) forms a broad cone of drooping branchlets. It is particularly useful where dense evergreen foliage is wanted to provide cover and texture.

factfinder

height	up to about 33 ft. (10m)
hardiness	zone 4
aspect	full sun to partial shade
soil type	fertile, free draining
soil pH	acid to neutral
country of origin	Japan (species)

The bright yellow foliage of 'Filifera Aurea' (far left) is similar in texture to 'Filifera' (left) but can be used to provide a highlight, particularly in winter. It is rather slower growing and ultimately smaller, growing to little over 6 ft. (2m).

51

The leaves are glossy green above with paler undersides and often turn yellow in fall.

Chionanthus virginicus
Fringe tree
Oleaceae

Although often referred to as a large shrub, this usually multi-stemmed plant can grow to 26 ft. (8m) with a spreading form. Its main asset is its early summer flowers, arranged in upright panicles and unusual in having long, narrow petals. They are produced on 2nd-year wood even on plants as young as 3 or 4 years old. Although fairly short-lived, they are of great beauty with a pleasant scent and give rise to deep blue plum-like fruits that ripen by late summer. The untoothed leaves are variable in size and turn an attractive yellow in the fall.

It will grow on any fertile well-drained soil, though it thrives best in slightly acid conditions. It prefers full sun or moderate shade with a reasonable degree of shelter. Although lacking the all-year-round appeal needed to be a prominent specimen tree it is very effective grown in combination with other plants to produce seasonal variety. It has a reputation for being very difficult to propagate from cuttings.

The fruits of C. retusus *(above) are small, deep blue oval berries.*

The bark is pale gray or brown, developing an attractive craggy look with age.

Other trees

There are no listed cultivars of this species. Although the genus contains about 120 species, only one other is commonly seen in cultivation. The Chinese fringe tree, *C. retusus,* is similar in most respects to *C. virginicus* but usually has somewhat smaller leaves.

factfinder

height	up to about 26 ft. (8m)
hardiness	zone 4
aspect	full sun to partial shade
soil type	fertile, well drained
soil pH	acid (best) to moderately alkaline
country of origin	southeastern USA

*C. virginicus varies greatly in shape, sometimes
forming a broad spreading shrub (above).*

*In early summer the
branches become covered
in the abundant scented
flowers. These are
produced on 2nd-year
wood, so care must be
taken when pruning to
allow for the next
year's flowering.*

Cladrastis kentukea
(Cladrastis lutea)
American yellowwood

Leguminosae

Although this tree is best known for its pea-like flowers, longer-lasting interest comes from its beautiful foliage that forms a dense and broad canopy about 50 ft. (15m) high, making it rather too large for smaller gardens. However, where space can be found, it is worthy of a prominent position. Its fragrant flowers are white and hang from the branches in drooping panicles during early summer, providing a spectacular display. The large pinnate leaves are pea-green when young, turning in the fall to bright clear yellow. Unusually, the leaf spine (or rachis) often remains on the tree well after the leaflets have been shed. The bark is smooth and pale gray and the wood, from which the tree gets its name, is yellow and was once the source of a yellow dye.

This species can be grown in any fertile well-drained soil of moderately acid or alkaline pH. It is also known by the synonym *C. lutea*.

In fall the leaves gradually turn yellow, starting at the edges. The color often develops unevenly, creating attractive variegated patterns.

The leaves are pinnate with 7 to 11 broad, untoothed leaflets. New leaves have a yellow tinge but gradually darken with age.

The trunk (above) may develop low forks. Where a more upright form is wanted, formative pruning from a young age should be carried out (see page 19).

Other trees

In recent years the pink-flowered cultivar 'Perkin's Pink' (*C. lutea* 'Rosea') has become available. In other respects it is like the species. The only related species at all common in cultivation is *C. sinensis*. This medium-sized Chinese tree is similar in many ways to *C. kentukea* but has pink-tinged flowers that are produced a little later in the summer. It is less easily obtained than *C. kentukea*.

Young trees (right) soon develop a broad rounded crown. Careful consideration should be given to planting position to allow plenty of space for full development.

factfinder

height	up to about 50 ft. (15m) but usually less
hardiness	zone 4 (*C. sinensis* 5)
aspect	full sun
soil type	fertile, free draining
soil pH	moderately acid to alkaline
county of origin	southeastern USA
observation	considered to be resistant to honey fungus

The creamy white-margined leaves of C. controversa 'Variegata' provide opportunity to create interesting combinations with plants of contrasting foliage.

Cornus alternifolia
Pagoda dogwood

Cornaceae

One of the most ornamental shaped of small trees, this species can be identified by the tiered effect created by its horizontal branching habit. In early summer the creamy white flowers form above each branch layer, further emphasizing its shape. Its small purplish-black fruits form in clusters by mid-summer, and in the fall the leaves turn to shades of red. Although rarely more than about 20 ft. (6m) tall, it usually develops a single-stemmed tree-like form and makes an excellent specimen plant for a small garden. Its strongly horizontal lines can be used to good effect to provide contrast with narrow upright plants or other vertical features.

It prefers a moist, free-draining acid soil in a partially shaded location. Like some other dogwoods, it does not thrive in areas prone to drought.

factfinder

height	up to about 20 ft. (6m)
hardiness	zone 3 (*C. controversa*, 4)
aspect	partial shade
soil type	moist, well drained
soil pH	acid
country of origin	eastern North America
observation	not suitable for drought-prone areas

Other trees

Where space allows, the related Japanese species *C. controversa* (giant dogwood) provides a larger alternative. It has a similar shape to *C. alternifolia* but can grow up to 65 ft. (20m) with a broad spread. Both species have cultivars with variegated leaves: *C. alternifolia* 'Argentea' ('Variegata') and *C. controversa* 'Variegata.' These are typically about half the height of the species, with creamy-white margined leaves. Of the two, *C. controversa* 'Variegata' is the most reliable and, being smaller and slower growing than the species, is suitable even for small gardens.

The creamy white flowers of C. controversa 'Variegata' (above) form above the branch layers in early summer and combine superbly with the variegated leaves.

Similar in many respects to C. alternifolia, C. controversa (left) is a larger tree that can hold its own in larger landscapes. Its fresh new leaves are bright green, emphasizing the layered arrangement of the branches.

From a young age, trees begin to develop the characteristic layered branching habit (right) that makes this species such a valuable landscape plant.

Cornus kousa
Chinese dogwood
Cornaceae

Unlike many of the more shrubby dogwoods, grown for their winter stem color, this beautiful east Asian species develops into a small tree and has long been cultivated for its neat, compact shape, and multi-seasonal interest. It is best known for its creamy-white flower bracts that cover the branches in early summer like thousands of pointed crosses. These are followed by the edible, strawberry-like fruits that develop from the inconspicuous flowers and give the tree its common name. In the fall the leaves turn to glorious tones of red and orange. It is particularly attractive when given enough space and all-round sunlight to develop a natural, unimpeded shape, and ornamental branching structure.

Although able to survive on even poor alkaline sites, growth and general appearance are much better when grown in a fertile soil. Pruning is not necessary and is best avoided.

The flowers themselves are inconspicuous but are advertised by creamy-white bracts (above), sometimes pink-tinged at their pointed tips. They are arranged in fours and make a striking sight against a background of dark green leaves.

Under suitable conditions specimens like this one (above) develop with broad billowing masses of foliage. In early summer the flowers form an almost continuous layer above the foliage.

The fruits (right) are small red globes that resemble strawberries. They are held on long stalks, either upright or dangling depending on their size. The leaves are untoothed with glossy surfaces and tapering tips. In some years they turn red and orange in the fall.

factfinder

height	up to about 50 ft. (15m) but usually less
hardiness	zone 5 (var. *chinensis* 4)
aspect	full sun (best) or partial shade
soil type	fertile, well drained
soil pH	neutral to acid
country of origin	Japan, Korea

Other trees

C. kousa var. chinensis is a geographical variant that tends to grow a little taller and is renowned for its spectacular fall color. Its leaves are slightly larger than C. kousa and can be distinguished by the lack of downy tufts on the undersides. It is generally considered to be hardier than C. kousa. There are a small number of cultivars of this species. Of particular merit is C. kousa 'Satomi,' a form with pink flower bracts and leaves that color purple in fall.

There are several other tree species of Cornus with many more cultivars. Of particular note are those of the American species C. florida (flowering dogwood) and C. nuttallii (Pacific dogwood).

Mature trees often develop attractive bark (left). The surface peels in irregular flakes to expose paler underlayers.

Cornus mas
Cornelian cherry

Cornaceae

The flowers (above) are arranged in tiny clusters borne close to the naked stems. They are produced from late winter and often remain long into spring.

The common name of this species refers to the cherry-like fruits that ripen over the summer to bright red and are sometimes eaten as preserves. Its best-known feature is the small yellow flowers that pack the dense network of branches in late winter, long before the appearance of leaves. In addition, some years see a good display of fall color, with the leaves turning a deep plum red. It is variable in form from a large, rounded shrub to a small tree, with some plants having a tendency to sucker. If left uncontrolled, they develop into large clumps, ideal for screening or ground cover. It may also be pruned to restrict size or produce a more upright habit.

In contrast to many other *Cornus* species that perform best in acid or neutral conditions and a free-draining soil, this one is very tolerant of a wide range of soil types and pH, including damp clays. It is best in full sunlight.

factfinder

height	about 16-26 ft. (5-8m)
hardiness	zone 4
aspect	full sun
soil type	very tolerant
soil pH	very tolerant
country of origin	central and southern Europe, western Asia

Other trees

A number of cultivars have been developed to provide a range of leaf coloration. 'Variegata' has green leaves with white margins, while those of 'Aurea' are toned yellow. 'Aurea Elegantissima' ('Tricolor') is a smaller, slower-growing plant with yellow variegated leaves that require partial shade.

C. mas 'Variegata' (above) has white-margined variegated leaves that give it a conspicuous outline, particularly when grown against a background of dark foliage. It is also renowned for being free-fruiting.

Cornus mas is at its best in late winter and early spring (right), particularly with sunlight illuminating its golden flowers and bare branch structure. It may form a small tree or large multi-stemmed shrub and is best grown in an open location in full sun.

The flowers are individually tiny but borne in open panicles, held upright above the foliage. They persist through the fall, fading to smoky gray.

Cotinus coggygria
Smoke tree, Venetian sumach

Anacardiaceae

Few garden trees provide as diverse a range of texture and color as this spreading shrub or tree. From mid-summer onward the finely divided flower inflorescences form a smoke-like haze around the foliage. They persist well into the fall by which time their fading tones of fawn and pink are supplemented by a blaze of color from the turning leaves. Although rarely more than about 13 ft. (4m) tall, it spreads broadly to form an attractive billowing shape.

All species of *Cotinus* grow well on fairly poor, dry soils in full sun. Where conditions are kinder, fall color is often less intense. If a compact form is desired they may be pruned, although this is better done little and often in spring to avoid

The bark becomes flaky with age.

unsightly wounds and gaps in the foliage. Some forms can be persuaded to develop a tree-like form by a combination of training and formative pruning.

Other trees

The species has a number of cultivars that display a range of leaf and flower variations. 'Royal Purple' has deep purple leaves that turn red in fall and often remain on the plant until early winter. 'Atropurpureus' *(f. purpureus)* has green leaves and purple-gray flowers. Some of the most striking cultivars are those of the hybrid between this species and its North American relative, chittamwood *(C. obovatus)*. They tend to inherit their more upright form from the latter and are a good choice where a larger plant is required. *Cotinus* 'Grace' and 'Flame' both have pink flowers and superb fall leaf color.

The flower panicles are pale pink or fawn colored. They appear in mid- to late summer and surround the foliage like a haze of smoke.

factfinder

height	up to about 13 ft. (4m); hybrids 26 ft. (8m)
hardiness	zone 4
aspect	full sun
soil type	any (not too fertile)
soil pH	acid to moderate alkaline
country of origin	Europe, western Asia

Old trees develop considerable character. Their tendency to spread may either be controlled by pruning, or used to good effect.

The leaves turn a variety of colors in fall, from yellow to red and purple. Many cultivars have been selected for their fall tones.

Crataegus crus-galli
Cockspur thorn

Rosaceae

North America is well endowed with native species of hawthorn, and this is one of the best for gardens. It has the characteristic "lollipop" shape of a broad round or oval crown set on a short branchless trunk. This makes it valuable as a landscape tree, particularly when grown in an open position or in relation to plants of contrasting shape. The leaves are glossy green and renowned for their fine range of fall colors. White flowers are produced in abundant clusters in late spring and give rise to deep red fruits that often persist well into the new year. Impressive thorns up to 3 in. (7.5cm) long give the tree its common name. They also make it unsuitable for use in places frequented by children or close to walkways.

The species is renowned for its tolerance of dry soils. It prefers moderately acid conditions and full exposure to the sun. In some areas, fungal leaf rust can be a problem. Although rarely a threat to the plant's survival, it can greatly affect its appearance.

The shoots bear sharp spines up to 3 in. (7.5cm) long. The leaves have glossy upper surfaces and broaden toward their toothed tips.

The bark (above) is gray-brown, becoming increasingly cracked and scaly with age.

Other trees

C. crus-galli is one of the parents of the well-known hybrid *C.* x *lavallei*, best known for the form 'Carrierei.' This tree is far less fiercely armed than its parent and may be almost thornless. Its fruits are more impressive, being up to ¾ in. (2cm) in diameter and long retained. The leaves provide good fall color and have the additional benefit of remaining on the tree late into the winter.

factfinder

height	up to about 26 ft. (8m)
hardiness	zone 3 (*C.* x *lavallei* 4)
aspect	full sun
soil type	well drained
soil pH	moderately acid
country of origin	central North America
observation	susceptible to fungal leaf rust

C. x *lavellei 'Carrierei' (left) has elliptical leaves that last into early winter and provide excellent fall color. The fruit are up to ¾ in. (2cm) in diameter and ripen to red in late fall. C.* x *crus-galli (right) has a neat rounded habit, ideal as a compact specimen or for restricted spaces.*

'Paul's Scarlet' (above) is one of the most commonly seen cultivars. Its double flowers are deep pink.

Crataegus laevigata
English hawthorn

Rosaceae

In its native Europe this is one of the most popular cultivated species of hawthorn. It is most often seen in hedgerows but is also grown as a specimen, particularly in open situations where its shape can develop to the full. Although small in height, reaching no more than about 33 ft. (10m), it is broadly spreading, developing a thick crown of densely leaved branches. In late spring these become covered in a profusion of white, scented flowers. The resulting small red fruits are borne in early fall and are a rich food source for birds. In common with most other hawthorns, the branches are armed with thorns that make this species ideal for hedging but less so for areas used by children.

A major asset is its tolerance of adverse growing conditions, including both dry and waterlogged soils and a broad pH range. On the negative side is its susceptibility to fungal blight that can cause summer leaf loss, particularly in the USA. Although primarily of aesthetic significance, the disease can be persistent and difficult to remedy.

factfinder

height	up to about 33 ft. (10m)
hardiness	zone 5
aspect	full sun to partial shade
soil type	very tolerant
soil pH	acid to alkaline
country of origin	Europe
observation	prone to leaf blight

Other trees

A number of cultivars have been developed to provide a range of flower color and form. 'Paul's Scarlet' has deep pink double flowers, while those of 'Punicea' ('Crimson Cloud') are similarly colored but single and with a conspicuous white "eye" at their center. 'Plena' has double white flowers and 'Aurea' has yellow fruit. For foliage interest, 'Gireoudii' has leaves with a mottled variegation.

A number of different forms of C. laevigata are commonly grown in gardens. Among them is 'Rosea Flore Pleno' (right).

C. laevigata *(above) usually develops an irregular spreading crown on a single clear trunk. As well as its ornamental qualities, it makes a good hedging plant, able to tolerate regular trimming.*

The cultivar 'Plena' (above) has double white flowers. They nestle among the lobed leaves in mid- to late spring. The flowers of the cultivar 'Rosea Flore Pleno' (right) are double-headed and pink.

Crinodendron hookerianum
Chilean lantern tree

Elaeocarpaceae

Given a suitable climate and position, this is one of the most desirable of evergreen plants for gardens. It may develop into a small tree up to 26 ft. (8m) in height, but is just as often a large multi-stemmed shrub with a broadly conical shape. The unusual flowers for which it is best known resemble crimson bells or lanterns suspended from stalks. They bloom in late spring and are made all the more conspicuous by the dark background of glossy green leaves.

The only downside is the species' rather choosy climatic requirements. Acid soil, partial shade, and mild temperatures are all required, although the latter can be overcome to some extent by positioning close to a sheltering wall. Alternatively it may be grown in a large container and moved to a cool, frost-free location during the winter.

The bright crimson flowers have a waxy texture and resemble long-stalked lanterns. The narrow leaves are deep glossy green with a leathery texture.

factfinder

height	up to about 26 ft. (8m)
hardiness	zone 8
aspect	partial shade
soil type	moist, well drained
soil pH	moderately acid
country of origin	Chile
observation	only for mild locations

Other trees

Crinodendron patagua is the only other species of the genus. It is of a similar hardiness to *C. hookeriana* and differs mainly in its white rather than crimson flowers that are produced in late summer.

The flowers appear in late spring and soon hang in abundance from the branches (right). Although fewer in number, late flowers continue to appear through much of the summer and early fall.

The bark (above) is dark purple-brown, developing shallow fissures with age.

This species often forms a broad multi-stemmed tree (right) as wide as it is tall. Its evergreen habit makes it suitable for screening, but in cooler areas it is best sheltered from cold winds.

Cryptomeria japonica 'Elegans'
Japanese cedar

Cupressaceae

The female flowers develop on the shoot ends and ripen in the following year.

The foliage (below left) is fine and feather-like and is this tree's main attribute. During the spring and summer it is glaucous green, turning gradually to bronze in fall and winter.

In the wild, Japanese cedar is a large forest tree that reaches heights of over 160 ft. (50m). However, it has given rise to many cultivars of more moderate size suitable for gardens. 'Elegans' is a small bushy tree with fine-textured juvenile foliage that, in fall and winter, turns an impressive bronze color. It has a compact, broadly conical shape, particularly when grown in full sunlight, and makes a good landscaping plant in combination with other contrasting conifers.

It tolerates most soil types with a moderate pH range, but does not thrive in particularly dry conditions. Large trees may become prone to damage by heavy snowfalls and can be protected by tying the branches over winter.

factfinder

height	up to about 26 ft. (8m)
hardiness	zone 5
aspect	full sun ('Sekkan-sugi' partial shade)
soil type	moist, well drained
soil pH	moderately acid or alkaline
country of origin	Japan (species)

Other trees

'Sekkan-sugi' is a very different form of the species. The young foliage is creamy yellow and contrasts with the bright green of earlier growth. It grows slowly into a small tree of a similar size to 'Elegans' but is best grown in partial shade to avoid scorching the delicate foliage.

Old trees become large enough to display rusty-red fibrous bark (left).

C. japonica 'Elegans' (right) has a broad shrubby habit, most useful where masses of dense foliage are wanted.

The tubular flowers are bright orange and up to 2 in. (5cm) long. As they mature, they split and curl backward to reveal the style within.

Embothrium coccineum
Chilean firebush

Proteaceae

The beauty of this plant when in full flower is matched by few other garden trees. Its narrow tubular blooms are produced in early summer and provide a spectacular display of almost tropical brilliance. It is only really suitable for warmer areas and does particularly well in the moist sunny climate of southern California. In these conditions it grows rapidly into an upright tree or large multi-stemmed shrub about 30 ft. (9m) tall. Although naturally evergreen, the variably shaped leaves may be shed when grown in cooler-than-ideal conditions.

Its possible cultivation range may be extended by planting it in the shelter of a wall or other trees. It requires a moist but well-drained soil free of lime and, unless grown in full sun, has a tendency to become "spindly" and unstable. It has a reputation for being difficult to transplant when large and so container-grown plants of moderate size should be used.

Other trees

This is a highly variable species that occurs in a number of forms. The best known and most hardy is called *Lanceolatum* Group (*E. coccineum* var.

E. coccineum (below) often forms a spreading multiple-stemmed tree whose low branches provide an opportunity for close examination of its unusual flowers.

The untoothed leaves (above) vary greatly in shape and color. Although evergreen in the wild, they often adopt a deciduous habit when cultivated in cool areas.

lanceolatum). It has narrower leaves than *E. coccineum* and a greater tendency to lose its leaves in winter. Its best cultivar, 'Norquinco,' is known for the abundance of its flowers. *Longifolium* Group is similar to *Lanceolatum* but has longer, more persistent leaves. Although it has given rise to a small number of cultivars, they are by no means commonly available.

factfinder

height	up to about 30 ft. (9m)
hardiness	zone 8
aspect	sheltered, full sun
soil type	moist, well drained
soil pH	acid
country of origin	Chile
observation	hardy only in mild areas

Eucalyptus gunnii
Cider gum

Myrtaceae

The adult leaves (above) are up to 4 in. (10cm) long and quite unlike the juveniles in shape. They are stalked, with smooth waxy surfaces.

Where space allows, E. gunnii *may be allowed to grow to a medium-sized tree (below), with an open crown and attractive bark.*

Although not fully hardy in areas with severe winters, this is one of the best eucalyptus species for most cool temperate climates. It is commonly grown for its ornamental bark and foliage, both of which provide year-round interest. The juvenile foliage is particularly attractive, the leaves being rounded and silver-blue. More mature parts of the tree produce leaves of a completely different, but hardly less interesting, shape. The bark of the trunk and main stems peels irregularly to reveal a range of colored layers beneath.

In suitable conditions it can grow to over 65 ft. (20m), making it unsuitable for small gardens. It is included in this book due to its suitability for growing as a small multi-stemmed tree by regular hard pruning. Although seemingly drastic, this method of cultivation has the benefit of producing an abundant supply of new juvenile foliage and stems. The frequency of pruning depends on the

The juvenile leaves (above) are blue-gray, and rounded with no stalks. Repeated cutting back to the stump ensures a continuous supply of new foliage.

The bark (above right) is gray, and peels with age to expose a pale cream or buff underlayer.

desired size. Annual cutting gives a dense bush of young shoots, while less frequent pruning allows the development of larger stems with colored bark.

Like most eucalyptus, this species is tolerant of a wide range of soil types. Although preferring full sunlight, it benefits from shelter from cold winds during the winter. It is best grown from small container-grown stock as successfully transplanting larger plants can be difficult.

Other trees

Eucalyptus parvifolia is a somewhat smaller tree, growing to between 33 and 50 ft. (10 and 15m). It has similar leaves to *E. gunnii* and multi-colored peeling bark. It is particularly valuable for its ability to grow on thin soils overlying chalk, and has a similar hardiness to *E. gunnii*.

factfinder

height	variable depending on cultivation (see above)
hardiness	zone 7
aspect	full sun with shelter
soil type	any reasonably fertile
soil pH	moderately acid or alkaline
country of origin	Tasmania

Eucryphia glutinosa
Nirrhe

Eucryphiaceae

factfinder

height	up to about 33 ft. (10m); *E.* x *nymansensis* 50 ft. (15m)
hardiness	zone 8
aspect	partial shade
soil type	moist, well drained
soil pH	acid
country of origin	Chile
observation	suitable only for milder climates

This is a popular tree in European parks and gardens where its late summer flowers make a valuable contribution at an otherwise relatively bloomless time of year for trees. In other seasons its dark, glossy foliage is good for screening or providing a background to more ornamental specimens. The flowers themselves are as spectacular individually as when seen from a distance, crowded along the branches. In its native Chile it is an evergreen species, but in cultivation may be partially or completely deciduous depending on climate. If deciduous, the leaves often color to various shades of orange and red in the fall. It grows at a moderate rate into a small upright tree, retaining its lower branches and foliage even in shade.

The best conditions are a moist acid soil in partial shade and, in colder climates, the shelter of other trees. It particularly dislikes direct sun around its roots.

The fragrant flowers have 4 petals and delicate red-tipped stamens. They appear in late summer, surrounded by the dark green leaves.

Other trees

Somewhat larger and faster growing than *E. glutinosa* is *E.* x *nymansensis,* a hybrid between *E. glutinosa* and *E. cordifolia.* It is most often seen in the cultivar form 'Nymansensis,' originally raised in the garden at Nymans, Sussex, England. It is considered more tolerant of moderately alkaline soils than *E. glutinosa,* but in most other respects is similar.

E. x *intermedia* (*E. glutinosa* x *E. lucida*) is another attractive hybrid that forms a small tree up to 33 ft. (10m). It often flowers through late summer and into the fall. It is best known as the cultivar 'Rostrevor.'

The bark (above) is smooth and gray. E. glutinosa (right) often develops a multi-stemmed form with horizontally spreading branches. It thrives in the partial shade of larger trees.

The leaves (right) are pinnate with 3 to 5 leaflets. Their upper surfaces are dark glossy green and contrast with paler undersides. Although evergreen in the wild, they are often semi- or wholly deciduous in cultivation.

Euonymus hamiltonianus
Spindle

Celastraceae

The leaves of deciduous forms of the species tend to color early in fall. The range of tones is variable, with pink and red being most common.

One of the larger spindles, this species is particularly effective grown in a large specimen group. The spring flowers are small and inconspicuous but give rise in late summer to flamboyantly colored fruits that later combine with turning leaves to provide a dazzling display. It varies from semi-evergreen to deciduous depending on climate and plant origin, and usually develops a broadly rounded crown on a short single or multiple stem.

In common with other spindles one of its great assets is tolerance of adverse conditions, including poor alkaline or compacted soils. It will also grow in moderate shade, although fruiting is most abundant in full sun. Fruiting is also promoted by planting more than one specimen together to ensure fertilization.

Perhaps the most remarkable feature of the species is its bright pink fruit (below left) that open to reveal red or orange seeds. The bark (below right) is pale gray and smooth, becoming shallowly fissured with age.

One potential problem is its susceptibility to scale insect attack. This commonly reduces its vitality and amenity value and, in extreme cases, may be fatal. Although treatment is possible, it rarely results in satisfactory control; where this pest is particularly prevalent it is advisable not to plant this and other vulnerable spindles.

factfinder

height	up to about 20 ft. (6m)
hardiness	zone 4
aspect	full sun (best) to partial shade
soil type	very tolerant
soil pH	acid to alkaline, including shallow over chalk
country of origin	eastern Asia
observation	susceptible to scale insect attack

Other trees

This is a highly variable and inconsistently named species with a number of wild-occurring subspecies and varieties. Where predictable results are wanted plants should be chosen from named cultivars such as *E. hamiltonianus* 'Coral Chief' and 'Coral Charm.' Both have pale pink fruits with red arils and leaves that color yellow in fall. Of the two, 'Coral Chief' is considered the most tree-like form.

E. europaeus is a related species from Europe. Among its attractive cultivars is 'Atropurpureus,' with leaves that turn from purple to brilliant red in fall.

The leaves (right) are glossy green and are arranged in opposite pairs along the shoots. The flowers are greenish-white and are borne in small clusters in late spring.

E. hamiltonianus (above) usually forms a spreading multi-stemmed tree. It really comes into its own in fall when the leaves display a rich variety of colors.

Euptelea polyandra
Japanese euptelea

Eupteleaceae

An uncommon plant outside botanical gardens and arboreta, this Japanese tree is, nevertheless, very suitable for small gardens. Its foliage is the main feature of interest, the leaves providing a combination of attractive shape and color. They open with a copper tint, gradually turning green, and give excellent fall colors of red and yellow. The flowers, although individually small, mass in clusters along the branches in spring to give an overall red haze. This is a plant that may be regarded as a large shrub or small tree. It is usually multi-stemmed and broadly spreading and is particularly suitable as a dominant feature in a large shrub border.

The leaves are almost round, with irregular jagged teeth and a long tip. Those produced on young wood (above) have a bronze tone that contrasts with the green of others.

It succeeds in any moist, well-drained soil, preferring a sunny position. Obtaining plants may not be as easy as more common species, requiring reference to "plantfinders" or the Internet. However, for those looking for something unusual, this is an interesting and uncommon plant.

Other trees

Euptelea pleiosperma is the only other species in cultivation. It varies from *E. polyandra* in having less irregularly toothed leaves, and is considered inferior in fall color.

factfinder

height	up to about 20 ft. (6m); *E. pleiosperma* similar
hardiness	zone 6
aspect	full sun (best) to light shade
soil type	moist, fertile, and well drained
soil pH	moderately acid to alkaline
country of origin	Japan (*E. pleiosperma* Himalayas, western China)

The bark is dark brown, sometimes with an interesting speckled pattern of paler colors.

E. polyandra (right) frequently forms a multi-stemmed tree with a spread equal to its height. Early pruning may encourage a more tree-like habit, but its leaves are the main attribute.

The shape and color of the leaves combine to create an ornamental foliage that looks particularly dramatic in strong light (left).

The glossy leaves are ovate with wavy untoothed margins.

Specimens grown in an open location (below) develop a dense dome of foliage reaching to the ground on all sides. It is particularly effective positioned in front of pale or brightly foliaged trees such as golden yew.

Fagus sylvatica 'Purpurea Pendula'
Weeping purple beech

Fagaceae

Of the numerous cultivars of European beech, this is one of the few small enough to be suitable for small gardens. It forms a short, mushroom-topped tree whose height depends on the level to which the weeping portion is grafted to the straight-stemmed rootstock. This varies from about 6–16 ft. (2–5m), enough to allow the deep purple-leaved branches to form an impressive cascade of foliage right down to the ground. It is hardly less dramatic in the winter when the absence of leaves reveals a basket-like network of descending branches. It has the additional benefit of being very tolerant of soil type and pH, though not suitable for sites experiencing prolonged drought. In common with other grafted plants, it has a tendency to revert to a normal form and upright shoots ascending from the dome-topped crown should be quickly pruned out to prevent the habit developing.

In a small garden situation this plant makes a strong landscape feature. Careful positioning provides endless opportunity for combination with plants and features of contrasting shapes, colors, and textures.

Note: This cultivar should not be confused with the green-leaved cultivar 'Pendula,' a massive tree quite unsuitable for small domestic gardens.

factfinder

height	about 6-16 ft. (2-5m), depending on height of graft
hardiness	zone 5
aspect	full sun to light shade
soil type	any except extremes of wet or dry
soil pH	any
country of origin	Europe
observation	tendency to revert to a non-weeping form

The new leaves (above) are variously colored gold, bronze, and green, gradually turning dark purple with age (left). In fall, leaves often turn to red.

Ficus carica
Common fig

Moraceae

Best known for its edible fruits, this tough little tree is also worth consideration as a garden specimen for its attractive foliage. Although not fully hardy in colder areas, it thrives when planted in the shelter of a sunny wall, even when rooted in a dry, rocky, and impoverished soil. It can reach a height of 33 ft. (10m), but may require the support of a trellis or other structure to maintain this kind of growth. Its deciduous leaves are fleshy and lobed and are joined in summer by golf-ball-sized fruits that gradually swell and turn from green to purple-brown. If left unpicked, they remain on the plant through the winter providing almost year-round interest. They are also delicious to eat, but require warmth and sun to form and ripen fully.

The fruits start green and gradually change to purple or brown as they swell. The cultivar 'Brown Turkey' (above) is self-fertile and a prolific fruit producer.

factfinder	
height	up to about 33 ft. (10m)
hardiness	zone 7
aspect	full sun and shelter
soil type	any except wet
soil pH	moderately acid to alkaline
country of origin	western Asia
observation	sap can cause skin irritation in sunlight

It is a great plant for growing up a trellis alongside a patio or other recreational area of the garden to provide shade as well as foliage interest. In milder coastal areas it can also be planted to give shelter, being tolerant of exposure and salt spray.

Other trees

This is the only fig tree hardy enough to grow in cool temperate climates. The wild form of the species requires pollination by wasps in order to produce fruit, whereas most plants in cultivation have been bred to fruit without the need for pollination. 'Brown Turkey' is the form most commonly grown, and has been selected for the quality and quantity of its figs.

Untrained, F. carica (below right) often forms a low spreading shrub with masses of lush foliage. It thrives in the poor dry soils frequently found close to houses, and is happy next to a warm wall.

The dark green, boldly lobed leaves (above) are up to 12 in. (30cm) in length and width with shiny upper surfaces. As well as being beautiful in themselves, they provide endless opportunity for contrasting with more delicately foliaged plants.

The fruit (above) are green capsules with 4 wings and a pointed beak. They are up to 2 in. (5cm) long, and hang in clusters through late summer and fall.

Halesia tetraptera (Halesia carolina)
Carolina silverbell (snowdrop tree)

Styracaceae

Despite its suitability for a range of garden situations, this beautiful species remains an uncommon sight in cultivation. Its common names describe the snowdrop-like flowers that emerge at about the same time as the new leaves in spring and hang in clusters along the branches. They are followed in early fall by attractive green fruits that are unusual in having 4 distinct "wings" running from top to bottom. Although not particularly noted for its fall color, in good years it displays a subtle tint of yellow. It grows to a height of about 33 ft. (10m) with a broad conical crown, often developed from more than one trunk.

It thrives best on a moist acid soil and is adaptable enough to grow in the partial shade of other trees or alone as a single specimen in full

factfinder

height	up to about 33 ft. (10m)
hardiness	zone 5
aspect	full sun to partial shade
soil type	fertile, moist
soil pH	neutral to acid, lime free
country of origin	southeast USA

sunlight. No pruning is required, but where necessary to limit size this should be carried out after flowering.

Other trees

Halesia monticola (mountain silverbell) is a closely related species that is sometimes considered so similar to *H. tetraptera* not to warrant separate species status. *H. monticola* var. *vestita* is renowned for its larger flowers, sometimes tinged pink. The cultivar 'Rosea' has more reliably colored pale pink flowers. *H. diptera* is a smaller, more shrub-like species distinguished by its 2-winged, rather than 4-winged, fruits.

If left unpruned, H. tetraptera (left) naturally develops an elegant shape with branches sweeping down to the ground. Pruning should be limited to removing dead and crossing branches. The flowers (right) are produced at about the same time as the new leaves from mid to late spring.

The bell-shaped flowers (left) are white, sometimes flushed pink, with orange anthers. They hang in clusters along the undersides of shoots. The leaves are finely toothed with pale hairy undersides when young.

The scented flowers (above) have 5 petals, and are borne in clusters from mid-summer.

Hoheria glabrata
Mountain ribbonwood

Malvaceae

Although one of the hardiest species of *Hoheria*, this small New Zealand tree or large shrub is only really suitable for milder areas. It does well in California and southern USA and looks a picture, particularly in mid-summer, when its arching branches are laden with sweetly scented flowers. It often has a multi-stemmed and spreading form but can, if desired, be encouraged into a more tree-like shape by selectively pruning some stems.

At the limit of its hardiness it may be successfully grown by planting in the shelter of a sunny wall or partial shade of lightly foliaged trees. It prefers shelter from cold winds and a deep, moist soil. It is particularly suitable for growing close to a well-used patio or path where its delicate foliage and flowers can be appreciated at close range.

Other trees

H. sexstylosa is an evergreen species, similar in hardiness to *H. glabrata*. Its flowers are smaller but no less attractive and are produced in late summer or early fall. *H.* 'Glory of Amlwch' is a cultivated form of the hybrid between the two species and a little larger and more tree-like than either parent. It may be evergreen or deciduous depending on climate, and is noted for its large and abundant flowers.

'Glory of Amlwch' (below) is a popular hybrid cultivar that combines semi-evergreen foliage with good flowering and a more tree-like form.

H. sexstylosa *(above) is an evergreen species that forms a small multiple-stemmed tree. Its small flowers are produced in abundance from late summer.*

factfinder

height	up to about 26 ft. (8m)
hardiness	zone 9
aspect	full sun or partial shade
soil type	moist, well drained
soil pH	moderately acid to alkaline
country of origin	New Zealand
observation	hardy only in warmer areas

Ilex aquifolium
English holly
Aquifoliaceae

The combination of glossy leaves and red berries makes
I. aquifolium *one of the most irresistible of winter-interest trees for the garden. The bark (below) is pale gray and smooth, often with interesting lumps.*

The glossy, often strikingly patterned, foliage and winter berries of this popular evergreen make it one of the most useful of all small trees for garden use. Although the species may occasionally grow to over 50 ft. (15m) in height, it is usually much smaller, particularly the cultivars. It is a plant of cool, moist conditions, tolerant of a range of soil types but susceptible to drought and extreme cold. In Europe it is often grown close to the sea for its ability to withstand severe exposure.

Its evergreen habit and prickly leaves make it particularly suitable for hedging, but pruning must begin early for this to be successful. Left unpruned, its strong outline and coloration make it a natural specimen tree. In common with most other hollies it is dioecious, having separate male and female plants. To ensure pollination and fruit production, berry-producing females must be grown within about 100 ft. (30m) of a male plant. Determining the sex of seed-raised plants can only be done after several years.

Note: This species thrives in the cool climate of the Pacific northwest and regenerates naturally from seed. It should not be grown where there is a danger of invasion into surrounding forest habitats. In these situations male cultivars only should be planted.

Other trees

European breeders have created a long and widely varying list of cultivars based mainly on leaf variation and berry production. 'Argentea Marginata' is a female variety with white-margined leaves. 'J.C. van Tol' has the great advantage of being a self-fertile female, able to produce its abundant berries without a male. There are also yellow-berried and weeping forms such as 'Bacciflava' and 'Pendula' respectively.

factfinder	
height	typically about 33 ft. (10m), sometimes more; cultivars variable
hardiness	zone 6
aspect	full sun to deep shade; variegated cultivars prefer good light
soil type	any moist, fertile soil
soil pH	moderately alkaline to acid
country of origin	Europe, north Africa, western Asia
observation	leaf miners are a common pest and should be treated early

The leaves of 'J C van Tol' (above) are almost spineless. The berries change from yellow-green to red as they ripen.

The strikingly variegated leaf margins of 'Argentea Marginata' (above) are emphasized by their sharp teeth. Grown in the open, I. aquifolium *(right) may develop a broad rounded shape. Its evergreen foliage and attractive berries make it a valuable tree for winter interest.*

Ilex opaca
American holly
Aquifoliaceae

This species plays a similar horticultural role in eastern USA to *Ilex aquifolium* in Europe. It is a little hardier than that species and less invasive, making it more suitable where this is a problem. Its glossy, spined leaves and red fruit are its main attributes, but many of its numerous forms produce trees with an attractive conical shape worth growing for that alone. Unfortunately its slow growth rate means a long wait if a sizeable specimen tree is wanted. It is ideally suited to planting in groups of varying shape and leaf color, or for accompanying ornamental deciduous trees to provide winter interest.

It requires a moist, acid soil, and although hardy in all but the coldest areas, suffers from desiccating winter winds. Leaf miner insects may be a problem, producing unsightly leaf blotching, and infected leaves should be removed and destroyed each spring.

The evergreen leaves are up to 4in. (10cm) long and spiny. Their upper surfaces are matte green, often with a slightly variegated vein pattern.

The berries may be almost ⅜ in. (1cm) across and vary in color depending on the cultivar. Those of the species (above) start yellow or orange and ripen to red.

Other trees

In the USA an estimated 1,000 cultivated forms of the species have been named. Many have a limited regional availability and some may be more suited to particular climatic conditions than others. 'Canary' is a yellow-fruited cultivar developed from the wild-occurring and commercially available form *xanthocarpa*. For variegated foliage and berry production, 'Steward's Silver Crown' has cream-edged leaves and only grows to about 20 ft. (6m). 'Jersey Princess' and 'Croonenburg' are both renowned for their berry production, the latter being self-fertile. 'Howard' is a nearly spineless plant with a columnar habit.

The dense evergreen foliage (left) is particularly good for screening purposes. Trees may be regularly trimmed to form a hedge.

I. opaca characteristically forms a broad column or pyramid of dark foliage (right), ideal as a background for smaller more decorative plants.

factfinder

height	about 33–50 ft. (10–15m) but very slow (most cultivars much less)
hardiness	zone 5
aspect	full sun to light shade
soil type	moist, well drained
soil pH	acid
country of origin	east and central USA

Juniperus scopulorum
Rocky Mountain juniper

Cupressaceae

The foliage forms irregular fronds, composed of tiny scale-like leaves closely pressed to the shoots.

Junipers form one of the most useful groups of conifers for use in the garden. This species is a good example, providing all-season interest with its strong symmetrical outline and evergreen foliage. In the garden situation it is most often seen as one of the many cultivars created to exploit the species' natural variability in shape, color, and foliage texture. As a species, it grows to a height of about 40 ft. (12m), with a narrow conical shape that allows it to fit into limited spaces. Its bark is red-brown with a tendency to peel with age, providing additional interest.

It shares with other junipers a tolerance of alkaline soils and, originating in the Rockies, is very hardy. On the downside is its susceptibility to some of the characteristic diseases of junipers, including Phomopsis canker.

factfinder

height	up to about 40 ft. (12m); cultivars vary down to dwarfs
hardiness	zone 3
aspect	full sun to light shade
soil type	well drained
soil pH	very tolerant
country of origin	western North America
observation	disease susceptible

Other trees

This and other species of juniper have given rise to an array of cultivars that provide garden designers with a rich choice of color and shape. *J. scopulorum* 'Skyrocket' is one of the best-known forms, its name aptly describing its very narrow upright shape reaching a height of little over 16 ft. (5m). 'Blue Heaven' reaches a similar height with a broader conical shape, but is most notable for its striking blue foliage. Contrasting shape and texture is provided by 'Tolleson's Weeping,' a cultivar with an open, irregular habit and thread-like silver-blue foliage. Where a feeling of formality is wanted the Irish juniper, *J. communis* 'Hibernica,' forms a dense, regular column about 13 ft. (4m) tall.

The evergreen foliage varies greatly in color from dark green to blue-gray. The latter tones (left) help emphasize the tree's unusual shape.

J. scopulorum *'Skyrocket' (left) lives up to its name, with even fully grown specimens having a width of little over 3 ft. (1m).*

Koelreuteria paniculata
Golden rain tree

Sapindaceae

factfinder

height	about 26–40 ft. (8–12m)
hardiness	zone 5 ('September Gold' 6)
aspect	full sun
soil type	well drained
soil pH	acid to alkaline
country of origin	China

The leaves are pinnate with 11 to 13 deeply lobed leaflets. They open in late spring and usually have a red tinge when young, gradually turning dark matte green. In fall they turn yellow, orange, and red. Late summer flowers quickly develop into bladder-like fruits (top). The 3-sided capsules are brightly colored green and red when young, ripening to yellow-brown.

Too often overlooked as a garden plant, this small tree provides a wonderful combination of dazzling flowers, unusual fruits, and fine foliage. Its panicles of yellow blooms form in mid- to late summer and may, in a good year, be numerous enough to almost completely obscure the leaves from view. They give rise to surprisingly large lantern-like fruits that gradually turn from bright green through yellow to brown. The leaves sometimes color yellow in fall, but just as often fail to deliver and drop before turning. It grows to about 40 ft. (12m) in ideal conditions, usually with a single trunk supporting a broad, rounded crown.

Although tolerant of heat, drought, and a range of less-than-ideal soil types, it thrives best and grows most rapidly in a well-drained fertile soil with a moderate pH. It is hardy in all but very cold areas, but best flowering is achieved in warm, sunny conditions, and shade may sometimes result in die-back. Light pruning may be carried out on young plants to promote a central leader and encourage an upright shape, but it should be kept to a minimum on older trees. It makes an excellent specimen tree, open grown on a lawn or as a central feature in a paved area.

Other trees

The best known and by far the most common cultivar is 'Fastigiata.' It is slower growing than the species and develops into a narrowly columnar tree about 26 ft. (8m) tall. Although rare, it may be obtained from specialist nurseries or plant centers. 'September Gold' is a North American form that flowers later than the species, in early fall, and is considered slightly less hardy.

The bark is pale brown or gray, with an attractive pattern of shallow fissures.

K. paniculata usually develops with a single main trunk and broad open crown. It is best when given an open position in full sunlight to promote flowering.

Laburnum × watereri
Waterer laburnum
Leguminosae

The pea-like flowers of L. anagyroides are borne in long chains in late spring and early summer.

This tough and reliable garden favorite is often known by its alternative name of "golden chain" from the dangling racemes of pea-like flowers that bloom in early summer. It has an upright, often multi-stemmed habit with broadly arching branches from which the masses of lightly scented flowers hang. It is well suited to training over a framework above a patio or path to provide a combination of shade and blooms. Unlike the parent species, this hybrid produces few of the poisonous seeds that make all laburnums unsuitable for use in areas frequented by children.

It is a useful plant for growing in poor, dry, and shallow soils, and especially on chalk where few other trees will succeed. Although short-lived (around 15 to 20 years), it is easily established and quick growing and one of the most reliable trees for year-after-year flowering. However, the show of flowers is relatively short-lived (2 to 3 weeks) and it is best combined with plants providing interest at other times.

Other trees

The most common and probably best form is 'Vossii.' It bears its abundant flowers in long racemes, 20 in. (50cm) or more in length. The parent species, *L. anagyroides* and *L. alpinum*, have given rise to a range of cultivars. Of particular note are the pendulous varieties of each, forming low dome-shaped trees and both going by the name 'Pendulum.' *L. anagyroides* 'Aureum' is a selection with yellow leaves during summer. Although a fine sight, it is liable to reversion to green.

In early summer the broad horizontal branches become laden with flowers. Trees grown in smaller spaces may be pruned to a narrower shape, or trained over an arch or trellis.

'Vossii' (left) is the most common cultivar, selected for its long racemes of flowers. The leaves have three dark matt green leaflets.

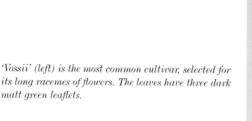

factfinder

height	up to about 20 ft. (6m)
hardiness	zone 5
aspect	full sun
soil type	very tolerant
soil pH	alkaline to moderately acid
country of origin	hybrid (more than one country)
observation	all parts of the plant are poisonous

Where space is at a premium, L. alpinum 'Pendulum' provides a very small weeping tree with a neat mushroom shape.

The bark (left) is dark gray and smooth. Old trees develop ridges and shallow fissures.

91

Typical flowers are pink, and borne in large panicles at the shoot ends.

Lagerstroemia indica
Crape myrtle

Lythraceae

In the southern states of the USA this species and its numerous cultivated and hybrid forms play a similar horticultural role to common lilac (*Syringa vulgaris*) in parts of Europe. In the species state it is a small tree with pink flowers and peeling bark, attractively mottled in a variety of colors. The flowers are produced on new growth and open in late summer or early fall. The leaves, although of no great merit during the summer, often provide good fall color. It requires a mild, sunny climate, particularly for successful flowering. It may be grown in cooler areas but requires the shelter of a warm wall. Alternatively, shrub-sized cultivars may be grown in containers and given greenhouse or conservatory protection during the winter.

There is much debate about the best pruning regime for crape myrtles. Most agree that light pruning after flowering in late fall and winter promotes young growth and good flower production in the following season. Over-aggressive pruning results in a misshapen plant and should be avoided. One major problem for the cultivation of this species is its susceptibility to fungal mildew.

factfinder

height	about 20-33 ft. (6-10m) cultivars dwarf to full size
hardiness	zone 9
aspect	full sun
soil type	well drained
soil pH	acid to moderately alkaline
country of origin	Korea and China
observation	for mild, sunny areas only

Numerous cultivars are available, providing a bewildering variety of flowers, including white ones (above). In the suitable conditions of a sheltered sunny garden (left), flowering is abundant and very showy.

Lagerstroemia are at their best in late summer and early fall when the branches are laden with blossom. The leaves later provide an impressive display of fall color.

The bark (below) has a habit of flaking, even from a young age, and is highly variable in color, particularly between the many hybrid cultivars.

Other trees

Literally hundreds of crape myrtle cultivars are now available commercially. The great breakthrough in their breeding occurred in the 1950s when the mildew-resistant species *L. fauriei*, introduced to the USA from Japan, was crossed with *L. indica* and prompted renewed interest from breeders. *L. indica* x *fauriei* hybrid cultivars now provide a broad spectrum of variety in size, shape, and color, requiring a specialist book to do them justice (see page 172). For small tree forms 'Natchez' has white flowers and rusty-colored bark, while 'Miami' has flowers of a delicate coral-pink shade and dark brown bark.

The fruits (above) are almost ⅜ in. (1cm) long and darken from blue-green to almost black.

Ligustrum lucidum
Tree privet

Oleaceae

Most privets are smallish shrubs, often seen as well-clipped hedges or screen planting. This species is capable of growing to 40 ft. (12m) tall on a suitable site and makes a fine specimen tree. Its glossy evergreen leaves are borne on a broad, rounded crown and are joined in late summer and fall by panicles of fragrant white flowers. These often persist for a considerable time and eventually give rise to purple-black berries. It shares its smaller relatives' tolerance of the rough-and-tumble of urban life, surviving everything from air pollution to poor compacted soils. Older trees often develop an attractively fluted trunk.

factfinder

height	about 26–40 ft. (8–12m)
hardiness	zone 8
aspect	full sun to partial shade
soil type	any
soil pH	acid to alkaline, including shallow over chalk
country of origin	China

Other trees

Two cultivars of the species are particularly worthy of inclusion. 'Excelsum Superbum' is of a similar size with leaves mottled pale green and edged with creamy yellow. It is sometimes considered less hardy than the species, requiring shelter from cold winds. The leaves of 'Tricolor' are narrower and pink-edged when young, gradually changing to pale yellow. *L. japonicum* is a smaller, more shrub-like species with lush evergreen leaves. It is very suitable for screen planting and has given rise to a number of cultivars in the USA.

The cultivar 'Excelsum Superbum' (left) is similar in size and shape to the species, but with attractively variegated leaves. The small white flowers (below) are very fragrant and borne in conical panicles at the shoot ends. The evergreen leaves open a bronze color, turning dark green and glossy.

Maackia amurensis
Amur maackia

Leguminosae

An unusual tree outside botanical collections, this relative of *Cladrastis* would nevertheless make a welcome addition to the list of plants regularly seen in streets and gardens. Although in no way spectacular, it makes an attractively shaped small tree with an exposed trunk and rounded crown. The pinnate leaves open a dusty pale green, gradually darkening as they mature. They are joined in early to mid-summer by lightly scented flowers, arranged in densely clustered upright racemes. The bark of young trees is a rich shiny brown, becoming coarser and peeling with age. It succeeds in most fertile, moist soils, preferring an open, sunny position. It makes an excellent shade tree, planted as a lawn specimen or by a patio or terrace.

The pinnate leaves have 9 to 13 leaflets that darken with age to deep matte green.

Other trees

The only other commonly grown species is *M. chinensis*. It varies little from *M. amurensis*, but is considered slightly less hardy (zone 4).

M. amurensis (above) typically forms an upright tree with a broad crown. It may be grown alone, or in combination with other species with contrasting foliage and flowering times.

The bark is red-brown, with conspicuous lenticels. Older trees develop an attractive, peeling texture.

The white flowers are borne in upright panicles in summer. Each one is less than ⅜ in. (1cm) long, with a pea-like structure.

factfinder

height	up to about 26 ft. (8m)
hardiness	zone 3
aspect	full sun
soil type	moist, well drained
soil pH	moderately acid to alkaline
country of origin	Manchuria

Magnolia grandiflora (cultivars)
Bull bay, Southern magnolia
Magnoliaceae

The leaves of all forms show a marked contrast between their glossy green upper surfaces and paler, often felted, undersides.

Few domestic gardens are big enough to accommodate a full-grown specimen of this tree, but it is included in this book for its smaller cultivars that display the species' best attributes on a more manageable scale. All have glossy evergreen leaves and creamy white flowers that emerge from conspicuous silky buds. Flowering time varies greatly from early summer through to fall depending largely on climate, with trees in cooler areas flowering latest. Since they are grown by grafting, they have a head start over seed-grown plants and some cultivars produce flowers much earlier than the 15 to 20 years taken by the species. The flowers give rise to woolly clusters of fruits that open in fall to reveal bright red seeds. They require moist, well-drained soils, but are tolerant of moderate alkalinity.

In its homeland climate of southeastern USA this tree thrives in all its forms, but will succeed in much cooler areas further north if provided with shelter. It is frequently seen trained against a wall, but is quite capable of growing into an unsupported specimen.

factfinder

height	cultivars about 13–33 ft. (4–10m)
hardiness	zone 7 ('Victoria' 6)
aspect	full sun to partial shade
soil type	moist, well drained
soil pH	acid to moderately alkaline
country of origin	southeastern USA

Other trees

The following cultivars all make small trees suitable for a modestly sized garden. 'Little Gem' is a slow-growing North American selection with a narrow, upright shape. The leaves are glossy above and felted rusty-brown beneath. Both they and the flowers are proportionately smaller than those of the species. Somewhat taller, with flowers and leaves more comparable with the species, is another North American variety, 'Victoria.' It is considered one of the hardiest forms. 'Goliath' has flowers that rival those of the species but are produced at a much younger age. Its leaves are shorter and broader, without the brown undersides.

The bark (far right) is pale gray, becoming flaky with age.

The fragrant flowers (right) are cup shaped, gradually opening to broad saucers up to 12 in. (30cm) across. The glossy evergreen leaves are thick and leathery, and vary in size from one cultivar to another.

In cooler climates M. grandiflora *may be grown against a house wall (above) to provide shelter and support. For most gardens, the small cultivars are a better choice.*

The cultivar 'Ferruginea' (left) is a compact form with typical flowers, but leaves covered on the undersides with a dense rusty-brown felt.

Magnolia x soulangiana
Saucer magnolia

Magnoliaceae

The flowers vary in shape from closed cups to broad saucers and lack distinct petals and sepals. The so-called tepals are white, suffused with pink toward the base.

Probably the best all-round magnolia for the small garden, the popularity of this hybrid is well deserved. It successfully combines flowers and foliage of great beauty with the ability to thrive in a range of growing conditions. It forms a broadly spreading and usually multi-stemmed large shrub or tree, varying greatly in height but often reaching up to 33 ft. (10m). It flowers reliably from a young age, producing its large, fragrant blooms in early spring before the emergence of the leaves. They are shaped like broad cups and vary in color from white to purple-pink.

Unlike its parents—that require an acid site—it tolerates heavy clay and even shallow alkaline soils, and is hardy in all but the coldest of climates. Large, tree-like forms make fine individual specimens, planted in a prominent position on a lawn. Those of a more shrubby, multi-stemmed shape are particularly effective planted in large single-variety groups.

'Alba Superba' (above) is an early flowering selection with pure white scented blooms. The flowers of 'Alexandrina' (right) have purple bases.

factfinder

height	about 13–33 ft. (4–10m)
hardiness	zone 4
aspect	full sun to light shade
soil type	very tolerant
soil pH	acid to moderately alkaline
country of origin	first cultivated in France

Other trees

This plant first came about from a cross produced in France in about 1820. The original clone was named 'Etienne Soulange-Bodin,' and it is this form that usually carries the hybrid name. However, the variability of the cross has allowed plant breeders to select and name numerous other cultivars that vary primarily in the color, shape, and timing of their flowers. 'Alexandrina' is one of the most popular and hardy forms, with tulip-shaped white flowers flushed purple at the base. The flowers of 'Brozzoni' are almost pure white and are among the latest to arrive and longest lasting. 'Lennei' is a broadly spreading, multi-stemmed shrub with dual-colored flowers, pink-purple on the outside and creamy white within. It is fast growing and late flowering. 'Grace McDade' is a North American selection, reputed to have the largest flowers of all at over 12 in. (30cm) across. They are white, tinged with deep pink. One of the earliest to flower is 'Alba Superba,' a popular European clone with almost pure white flowers.

The bark is smooth and gray, often becoming coated in algae and lichen.

Most plants develop a round spreading shape, with several stems and wide-spreading limbs. In early spring (above) the leafless branches become laden with flowers.

The flowers open to reveal both male and female elements (right). They later develop into knobbly fruits that ripen from green to pink.

Magnolia stellata
Star magnolia

Magnoliaceae

For those with very modestly sized gardens—but determined to have a magnolia—this species is ideal. It is both slow growing and small, usually no more than 10 ft. (3m) tall with a similar spread. Its dazzling white flowers emerge from conspicuous woolly buds in early spring and more than make up for its modest size. They tend to have a staggered opening time, lengthening the flowering period to over 2 weeks. Although one of the hardiest of magnolias, its early flowers are susceptible to late frosts and it benefits from some shelter. It prefers an acid or neutral soil but will tolerate a degree of alkalinity, and is better able than most species to survive hot, dry spells. It is frequently seen growing in small front gardens where larger trees would be out of scale or cause obstruction.

The leaves are relatively small for a magnolia, with dark upper surfaces and paler beneath. The fruits are knobbly clusters that change from green to red.

Other trees

Numerous cultivars are available, showing a range of flower shapes and colors. 'Centennial' is faster growing and more upright than the species, with pure white flowers made up of 25 to 32 long tepals. It was named to commemorate the 100th anniversary of the Arnold Arboretum in Boston. 'Water Lily' is a Japanese form whose many-petalled white flowers are said to be particularly fragrant and emerge from pink-flushed buds. A number of pink-flowering selections have been named, the best known of which is 'Rosea.'

The flowers of the cultivar 'Rosea' (below) have a pale pink tinge.

The typical flowers are pure white with many narrow tepals. They are produced in early to mid-spring and may be damaged by late frosts.

'Centennial' (left) is a selection grown for its unusual flowers. It has a more upright form than the species.

factfinder

height	up to about 13 ft. (4m)
hardiness	zone 4
aspect	full sun to partial shade
soil type	fertile, well drained
soil pH	acid to moderately alkaline
country of origin	Japan

Its modest size makes M. stellata (right) one of the best magnolias for very small gardens. It usually has a number of stems and a broad round crown.

Malus floribunda
Japanese crab apple

Rosaceae

The flowers have 5 petals and fade from pink to white. They appear in mid-spring with the small, finely-toothed leaves.

M. 'Golden Hornet' is an old but still popular ornamental selection with pink-flushed flowers. Its fruit (above) are up to 1 in. (2.5cm) across and deep yellow in color. They are produced in great abundance (right) and long retained.

The typical tree (far right) has a single stem supporting a round crown with dark angular branches. Its neat outline and clear trunk make it a suitable tree for a lawn or restricted space.

Despite its long history of cultivation, this old favorite can still hold its own among the ever-growing list of ornamental crab apple varieties. It is eminently suitable for the small garden, combining compact size and shape with ease of cultivation and disease resistance. It forms a small, usually single-stemmed tree, with a dome or umbrella-shaped crown, often wider than its height of about 20 ft. (6m). The flowers emerge from crimson buds in early spring and, although initially pink, soon become white. At their peak they mass along the branches forming an almost unbroken covering of blossom. The resulting fruits are miniature shiny yellow apples, often tinged with various degrees of pink or red.

Like other crab apples, it prefers a reasonably fertile site and a sunny situation. It will not thrive in over-wet conditions and flowering may be less abundant where the soil is too fertile. The species has stood the test of time partly because of its good resistance to the range of pests and diseases that afflict apples. However, it is not immune, with fireblight, scale, and scab among potential problems.

factfinder

height	up to about 20 ft. (6m)
hardiness	zone 4
aspect	full sun (best) to light shade
soil type	fairly fertile, well drained
soil pH	moderately alkaline or acid
country of origin	Japan
observation	susceptible to various common diseases of apples

Other trees

This species is usually considered a hybrid of unknown origin that has gained favor for its horticultural qualities. The popularity of flowering crabs for garden use has resulted in a wealth of hybrids and cultivars, selected for their ornamental value and disease resistance. They provide gardeners with enormous choice and selection is largely a question of personal taste and suitability for a particular situation. *Malus* 'Centurion' grows to about 20 ft. (6m) with an upright habit, rose-pink flowers, and small cherry-red fruits. 'Sugar Tyme' and 'Donald Wyman' have white flowers and red fruits that last into the winter. 'Golden Hornet' is an older selection and still one of the best for fruit production with abundant yellow apples. All these have good disease resistance.

Malus hupehensis
Tea crab apple

Rosaceae

The small apples (above) are less than ⅜ in. (1cm) across. They usually ripen from green to deep red (sometimes yellow) and remain long after the leaves. The fragrant flowers (below) are open white cups borne in loose clusters.

Although in many ways similar to *Malus floribunda*, this species is typically a rather taller tree with its ascending branches forming a more open, irregular crown. Its common name derives from the use of its leaves for tea-making in its native China. The pink flower buds open in late spring and give rise to clusters of long-stalked white flowers. By late summer the branches are covered in small, shiny apples that vary in color from deep cherry-red to almost pure yellow. They often persist long after the leaves have fallen to provide fall and early winter interest. The tree's multi-seasonal value is also enhanced by the habit of older plants to develop attractive gray and brown flaking bark.

Its ornamental spreading habit, and dislike for any more than light shade, make this tree suitable for an open location where its branches can stretch unhindered. Where pruning is necessary to remove untidy or over-long branches, it should be done during the summer, after flowering. It needs a well-drained soil but requires only moderate fertility. It is less resistant to fireblight than some other species and cultivars, and should not be grown in areas where the disease is a particular problem.

factfinder

height	up to about 33 ft. (10m)
hardiness	zone 4
aspect	full sun (best) to light shade
soil type	fertile, well drained
soil pH	moderately acid to alkaline
country of origin	China, Japan
observation	susceptible to fireblight

Other trees

The only commonly listed cultivar is 'Rosea,' a form differing mainly in its pale pink, rather than white, flowers.

Malus sargentii (Sargent crab apple) is a very small tree or large shrub whose height of about 10 ft. (3m) is usually much exceeded by its spread. It has white flowers and small, pea-like red fruits that are retained through the fall. It has a reputation for very good disease resistance. Where space is really at a premium, the cultivar 'Tina' is even smaller, growing to only about 5 ft. (1.5m) tall.

M. sargentii (left) forms a low spreading tree, suitable for very small gardens. It produces masses of white, yellow-anthered flowers. The bark (right) becomes increasing fissured with age. The surface is dark brown, sometimes flaking to reveal rust-brown beneath.

From a young age (right) trees develop a broad open crown, allowing plenty of space for flowers.

Morus nigra
Black mulberry

Moraceae

The fruit ripen from green to dark red and are excellent to eat. They are held close to the stems in small clusters.

Few small trees have as much character as a well-grown specimen of this western Asian species. It is somewhat smaller and less hardy than its Chinese counterpart, the white mulberry (*Morus alba*), but produces fruit of greatly superior eating quality. It rarely reaches 33 ft. (10m) in height, with spreading branches that gain a similar width and form a broad, rounded crown. The bark soon becomes ruggedly contorted, adding to the tree's aged appearance. Its raspberry-like fruits are produced in abundance and are excellent eaten fresh or preserved—just as well considering the mess they make if not picked and allowed to fall to the ground! The large, deciduous leaves remain unmolested by insects or other pests and cast a deep, cool shade.

Although a tree of rich, well-drained soils, it tolerates the combined urban perils of salt spray (from de-icing roads) and pollution, and is renowned for its longevity. In common with other species of mulberry, it can be easily propagated from hardwood cuttings inserted directly into the open ground.

Other trees

For cooler climates of zone 5 and below, and where space allows, *Morus alba* is a more suitable tree. It grows to a height of up to 50 ft. (15m) but, unlike *M. nigra*, has a number of cultivars more suitable for small gardens. 'Pendula' forms a very small, dome-shaped shrub with a crown of weeping branches. For a similar shape without the problems of fallen berries, 'Chaparral' and 'Urbana' are fruitless selections. Fruitless tree forms are also available, including 'Stripling.' These are particularly recommended for areas of the USA where white mulberry may be considered an invasive pest.

factfinder	
height	up to about 33 ft. (10m); *M. alba* 50 ft. (15m)
hardiness	zone 6 (*M. alba* 4)
aspect	full sun to partial shade
soil type	fertile, well drained
soil pH	very tolerant
country of origin	western Asia

The leaves are heart-shaped and up to 6 in. (15cm) long. They are roughly hairy beneath, with jagged teeth.

M. nigra *(above) develops into a broadly*
spreading tree, often wider than it is tall.
Its long horizontal branches often layer
along the ground and take root.

The bark (right) is dark
orange-brown, and
acquires an interesting
gnarled appearance with
deep fissures.

Nyssa sinensis
Chinese tupelo

Cornaceae

The leaves (above) are up to 8 in. (20cm) long with glossy upper surfaces. They are tinged red and bronze when young, and turn red, orange, and yellow in fall.

Less well known than its larger American relative *Nyssa sylvatica*, this species is a more suitable size for small gardens. It is variable in height but tends to be smaller in cultivation than in its native China, usually developing into a small tree or large shrub with a broad conical crown. Its main asset as a garden specimen is its superbly colored foliage. The new leaves flush brilliant red, gradually turning green through the growing season before changing in fall to a spectrum of colors from yellow through red and orange to purple. The gray bark cracks and flakes with age, providing additional interest.

In common with other members of the genus, it needs a moist, acid soil in full sun or partial shade. It is best grown from small plants as it becomes increasingly difficult to transplant successfully with age. Although uncommon in cultivation, it

factfinder	
height	up to about 26 ft. (8m), but very variable
hardiness	zone 7 (*N. sylvatica* 4)
aspect	full sun to partial shade
soil type	moist, but well drained
soil pH	acid
country of origin	China

can be obtained through specialist nurseries. In larger gardens a closely spaced group creates a really dramatic fall color spectacle.

Other trees

Black tupelo, *Nyssa sylvatica*, is a medium-sized tree growing to a height of about 65 ft. (20m). Its leaves are typically broader and more rounded than those of *N. sinensis* but display a similar range of fall colors. It is hardier than its Chinese relative and more generally available.

Where space allows, N. sylvatica (left) provides a readily available alternative. It combines superb fall color with a graceful shape and attractively fissured bark.

The bark of N. sinensis (above) is gray-green in color and becomes flaky with age. Even from a young age, N. sinensis (right) forms a rounded crown of foliage.

In fall leaves turn unevenly to shades of red and yellow.

Oxydendrum arboreum
Sourwood

Ericaceae

Although common in its native range in southeastern USA, this small deciduous tree has not become a regular sight in urban and domestic landscapes. This is surprising, considering its many assets. It typically develops into a broadly conical tree with branches that descend toward their tips, giving it a graceful appearance. The creamy white flowers are borne in curved panicles from the ends of the shoots in mid- to late summer, and have a passing resemblance to those of *Pieris*. They last for many weeks, sometimes remaining until the glossy green leaves begin turning to yellow, red, and purple in the fall.

factfinder	
height	up to about 33 ft. (10m)
hardiness	zone 5
aspect	full sun to light shade
soil type	moist, moderately fertile
soil pH	acid
country of origin	southeastern USA

The dark glossy leaves (below) are up to 8 in. (20cm) long with fine teeth.

It requires similar conditions to those enjoyed by its ericaceous relatives like rhododendrons, namely a moist, acid soil in full sun or light shade. It has a reputation for being difficult to propagate and transplant, and is best grown from small container-grown plants. Its ornamental shape, combined with multi-season interest, makes it a natural specimen plant for a prominent position.

O. arboreum may form an upright tree or broad shrub (below). The flowers are held high in the crown from mid-summer, and often coincide with the early signs of fall color.

The leaves turn a variety of colors in fall, depending on weather and soil conditions. Tones of red, yellow, and orange may be displayed all at once on the same branch or even leaf.

Parrotia persica
Persian ironwood
Hamamelidaceae

As well as being one of the best small trees for multi-seasonal interest, Persian ironwood is also easy to grow and tolerant of a range of soil conditions. It varies greatly in height and shape, with two fairly distinct forms recognizable. Most plants in cultivation grow into a low and broadly spreading tree, wider than their eventual height of about 26 ft. (8m). In its native northern Iran (and sometimes in cultivation) it develops a more irregular upright shape and greater height. In both cases its slow growth rate is adequately compensated for by its early appeal. The large, beech-like leaves form an almost unbroken canopy around the descending branches and put on a spectacularly vivid display of fall color. The transformation often starts early and spreads unevenly over the crown, turning it to glorious shades of red, yellow, and orange. The bright red flowers appear in late winter and, although small, are made more conspicuous by the absence of leaves. The flaking bark of older trees develops a dappled pattern reminiscent of London plane.

Although preferring a well-drained fertile soil, the species succeeds in less amenable conditions and is very tolerant of lime. It may be pruned to reveal

The small flowers lack petals but are made conspicuous by their crimson anthers. They appear in late winter on bare branches and contribute to the tree's all-year-round appeal.

The bark flakes in irregular patches, revealing a range of subtle tones.

its lower trunk or control sideways growth, but spreading forms tend to resist all attempts at encouraging a more upright habit.

Other trees

The variation in shape shown by the species is reflected in its cultivars. The most common is 'Pendula,' a form that emphasizes the spreading habit to produce a mushroom-shaped mound no more than about 10 ft. (3m) high. 'Vanessa' is a far less easily available selection that develops a more tree-like shape and has red shoots.

factfinder

height	up to about 26 ft. (8m), occasionally much more
hardiness	zone 4
aspect	full sun (best) to light shade
soil type	fertile, well drained (best), but tolerant
soil pH	acid to alkaline
country of origin	Iran

Most trees develop a low spreading shape (right) with dense foliage falling right to the ground.

The leaves are up to 3 in. (7.5cm) long with fine points and teeth. The edible berries are egg shaped and ripen to a bright glossy red.

Photinia villosa
Oriental photinia

Rosaceae

This deciduous photinia may be described as a large shrub or a small tree. In either case it has much to offer the small garden. It usually develops a broad, irregularly shaped crown from a number of stems, and has a width similar to its height of about 13 ft. (4m). A more tree-like form can be encouraged by early selective pruning to favor one or more dominant stems. Its white *Crataegus*-like flowers appear in late spring and, although numerous, are outshone by the resulting fruits. These are shiny red berries that ripen in early fall and later combine with the orange and yellow tones of the turning leaves to provide a fine show of color.

It is a plant for moist, acid soils and a sunny or lightly shaded situation. It can be very effective planted as an individual specimen or in a single-species or mixed group. In common with other species of photinia, fireblight can be a problem in some areas.

Other trees

Photinia davidiana is a strongly growing species that can reach a height of 33 ft. (10m). It tends to form a low-branching small tree with a broad rounded crown. Its lush evergreen leaves are particularly effective in fall when the older ones turn bright red before dropping. The flowers are borne on rounded heads in summer, and give rise to bunches of spherical red fruits. Its soil requirements are similar to those of *P. villosa*, and it too is susceptible to fireblight.

The fall leaves (above) are accompanied by the fruit.

The foliage is relatively late to color in fall (above), turning gradually to orange and red. P. villosa *may be either a single-stemmed tree (right), or more shrub-like (above). Early training can influence the final form.*

factfinder

height	up to about 13 ft. (4m)
hardiness	zone 4 (*P. davidiana* 6)
aspect	full sun (best) to light shade
soil type	moist, well drained
soil pH	acid
country of origin	Japan, Korea, China (*P. davidiana* China)
observation	susceptible to fireblight

The bark (left) is gray-brown, becoming fissured with age.

Pinus aristata
Bristlecone pine

Pinaceae

The needles are up to 1½ in. (4.5cm) long, and held in bundles of 5.

A tree of great character and longevity, the bristlecone pine has succeeded in making the transition from wild mountaintop to domestic garden. Its reputation for very slow growth is well deserved, and although it grows faster in cultivation than in the wild, trees of over 33 ft. (10m) are a rare sight—and of considerable age. Unlike many pines, it develops an interesting, irregular shape early on, making it a valuable plant for lending character to young gardens. Its short needles are glaucous green and often spotted with white resin. The cones are oval shaped and have scales that end in a bristle-like spine from which the tree gets its name.

The evergreen foliage and cones (below) provide interesting texture and color throughout the year.

It is a very adaptable species, succeeding even in poor, dry soils and a range of pH values. It is also very hardy and tolerant of extreme exposure. Its slow growth means that plants of any size are

factfinder	
height	rarely more than 33 ft. (10m), very slow growing
hardiness	zone 3 (*P. bungeana* 4)
aspect	full sun to light shade
soil type	any well drained
soil pH	very tolerant
country of origin	southwestern USA China (*P. bungeana*)

expensive and not always easy to obtain. However, it is well worth searching for a reasonable-sized, good-quality plant to provide quick effect.

Other trees

One of the most ornamental of all pines is the lacebark pine, *P. bungeana*, so named for its extremely ornamental bark. It is another fairly slow-growing species eventually reaching a height of up to about 50 ft. (15m). Although a little less hardy than *P. aristata*, it does well in dry soils, either acid or moderately alkaline.

Young trees (right) quickly develop an irregular shape. Slow growth and small size make this tree particularly suitable for the smallest gardens.

The bark of P. bungeana *(below) is its most prominent feature. Even fairly young trees begin to show the multi-colored flaking bark that gives the species its name.*

Pinus sylvestris 'Aurea'
Golden Scots pine

Pinaceae

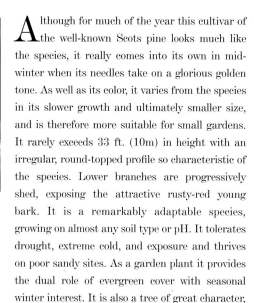

During the summer and into fall the cones develop and grow. The foliage remains green until the winter.

Although for much of the year this cultivar of the well-known Scots pine looks much like the species, it really comes into its own in midwinter when its needles take on a glorious golden tone. As well as its color, it varies from the species in its slower growth and ultimately smaller size, and is therefore more suitable for small gardens. It rarely exceeds 33 ft. (10m) in height with an irregular, round-topped profile so characteristic of the species. Lower branches are progressively shed, exposing the attractive rusty-red young bark. It is a remarkably adaptable species, growing on almost any soil type or pH. It tolerates drought, extreme cold, and exposure and thrives on poor sandy sites. As a garden plant it provides the dual role of evergreen cover with seasonal winter interest. It is also a tree of great character, with no two individuals being quite alike.

There is debate about the botanical status of this form of Scots pine. Various golden clones have been selected and are sometimes described under the general name Aurea Group or *forma aurea*.

The needles are about 2½ in. (7cm) long and held in pairs. From early winter they gradually turn from green to yellow from the tips inward. By late winter they are a bright uniform golden color.

factfinder

height	up to about 33 ft. (10m)
hardiness	zone 3
aspect	full sun
soil type	very tolerant
soil pH	very tolerant
country of origin	Europe (species)

The young bark flakes irregularly to reveal a range of rusty-red tones. Older trees develop deeply fissured bark.

Other trees

The species has given rise to many other cultivars from full-size trees to dwarfs suitable for the rock garden. 'Fastigiata' is a narrowly columnar tree that grows to a height of about 27 ft. (8m). It is variously known as the sentinel pine or pyramidal Scots pine. Slower growing but ultimately reaching a similar size is 'Watereri,' a form with conspicuously blue foliage. Where size is really at a premium, 'Beuvronensis' provides a miniature shrub version.

In the gloom of winter, the bright color and bold outline of Pinus Sylvestris 'Aurea' (right) makes a striking sight.

The flowers are borne in dense clusters close to the branches. They have 5 petals and, although pink when new, soon fade to almost white.

P. dulcis 'Macrocarpa' (below) forms a broad round crown with a short single trunk and ascending branches.

Prunus dulcis
Common almond

Rosaceae

Long cultivated for its edible fruits and ornamental qualities, the almond remains one of the most attractive and reliable spring-flowering trees for milder areas. It forms a small round-topped tree of about 26 ft. (8m) in height, though plants grown in colder areas tend to be smaller. Its flowers are produced in early to mid-spring before the leaves, and are a delicate shade of pale pink. The leaves are unusual for cherries, being narrow and willow-like in appearance. The green spherical fruits are about 2¼ in. (6cm) across and split open to reveal the familiar almond stone. They tend to be produced only in warmer areas, and are rarely as good as the commercially produced nuts.

This is a tree that can live to a great age and lend character and continuity to a garden. It should be given an open position in full sun, where its flowers can be fully appreciated. It requires a moist but well-drained soil of medium pH including moderately alkaline. Pruning is best avoided, but where necessary to remove diseased or dead wood should be carried out in summer. The species' only real drawback is its susceptibility to peach leaf curl, a fungal disease caused by the organism *Taphrina deformans*. Although copper-based fungicides are available, their use for ornamentals in the garden is not usually practical: the difficulties of application, expense, and environmental problems outweigh the likely benefits. In areas where it is a particular problem, more resistant cherries should be grown.

Other trees

One of the best-known cultivars for nut production is 'Macrocarpa.' Its flowers and fruit are both larger than those of the species. 'Roseoplena' is a double-flowered form, while 'Alba' has single white flowers.

factfinder	
height	up to about 26 ft. (8m)
hardiness	zone 7
aspect	full sun
soil type	moist, well drained
soil pH	acid to moderately alkaline
country of origin	western Asia to northern Africa
observation	susceptible to peach leaf curl

The flowers are produced before the leaves in early spring and stand out conspicuously on the bare branches (above).

The bark of P. serrula (far left) is bronze colored with a brilliant sheen. P. maackii (left) has glossy yellow or golden bark with a pattern of horizontal lenticels. The bark of both species peels attractively.

Prunus serrula
Tibetan cherry

Rosaceae

The leaves of P. maackii (above) are finely toothed and taper to a fine point. The fragrant flowers, although individually small, are borne in tight racemes at the ends of shoots.

One of the few ornamental cherries not grown for its flowers, this species' main asset is its attractive bark. It is a fairly fast-growing tree with a broad crown, reaching a height of about 26 ft. (8m). The main trunk often divides low into a few major limbs, each displaying the superb glossy red-brown bark. This develops on plants from as young as 5 years old, but takes at least as much again to become really effective. The flowers are produced at about the same time as the emerging leaves in mid- to late spring. They are small and white and inconspicuous in comparison to cherries grown for their blossom. They give rise to small red cherries, borne in pairs on long stalks.

The requirements of the species are similar to those of most flowering cherries. Although tolerant of fairly shallow alkaline soils, it does not thrive in those with a tendency to become very dry or wet. It performs best in a sunny position with a degree of shelter. From the garden design perspective, it should be grown where its bark can be appreciated at close range. It is particularly good in a small raised bed, centrally positioned in a patio or other well-used area.

Other trees

Another species known for its attractive bark is Manchurian cherry, *Prunus maackii*. It is a vigorous tree that can reach over 40 ft. (12m) in height, with a broad conical shape. Its glossy bark is amber colored, often flaking in large sheets. The white flowers are arranged in dense clusters on old shoots in late spring. It is a very hardy species that does not thrive in warmer areas above about climatic zone 7.

factfinder

height	up to about 26 ft. (8m), occasionally more
hardiness	zone 6 (*P. maackii* 2)
aspect	full sun
soil type	moist, well drained
soil pH	very tolerant
country of origin	western China (*P. maackii* Manchuria, Korea)

P. serrula forms a broad-crowned tree. Pruning should be limited to removal of dead or diseased wood and carried out in mid-summer.

Prunus x subhirtella
Higan cherry, spring cherry

Rosaceae

The flowers are produced in early spring before the arrival of leaves. They emerge from deep pink buds and have delicately notched petals.

This highly variable tree, though unknown in the wild, has a long history of cultivation in its Japanese homeland. Like many of the ornamental cherries from that country, it has been refined over the centuries to produce a number of forms that provide gardeners with a wealth of choice in flower color and shape. In its non-cultivar form it occasionally grows to a medium-sized tree up to about 40 ft. (12m) in height, but is usually much smaller. Its small pale pink flowers are produced before the leaves in spring and are a sight of great beauty. The leaves that follow are bronze-tinged when young, changing to deep green, and finally yellow in fall.

All forms of the tree have similar requirements, being tolerant of all well-drained soils, including lime. It is susceptible to fungal blossom wilt, a disfiguring ailment that is particularly prevalent where a number of cherries are grown in close proximity. Pruning should be avoided except to remove dead or diseased wood, and then carried out in mid- to late summer when "gumming" may help to prevent disease entry.

The cultivar 'Pendula' forms a graceful weeping tree with a slender habit. Its flowers, though abundant, are relatively small and pale.

factfinder

height	up to about 40 ft. (12m), but some cultivars less
hardiness	zone 4
aspect	full sun (best) to light shade
soil type	moist, free draining
soil pH	very tolerant, including lime
country of origin	Japan (garden)

The flowers vary in their intensity of color from one tree to another. Typically they are a soft pink (above).

The variability and uncertain origin of higan cherry has also led to considerable ambiguity in naming, but it is now usually considered to be of hybrid origin.

Other trees

P. x *subhirtella* 'Autumnalis' is a smaller tree up to about 26 ft. (8m) tall with a similar width. Its white or pale pink flowers are produced unpredictably between fall and spring, and may be even be seen on a mid-winter's day. 'Pendula Rosea' and 'Pendula Rubra' are weeping trees, usually wider than their height of about 16 ft. (5m). Both flower in early spring and vary mainly in flower color—rose pink in 'Pendula Rosea,' deeper pink in 'Pendula Rubra.' 'Stellata' is an upright tree whose flowers have pointed petals, giving them a star-like appearance. Along with the two previously named cultivars, it is sometimes attributed to *P. pendula* and given that name.

Prunus x subhirtella
'Pendula Rubra' (above)
is a commonly seen
cultivar that combines
an ornamental shape
with superb flowers. It is
grafted onto a straight
trunk and its weeping
branches form a broad
dome, often wider than
its height.

The cultivar 'Stellata'
(left) is a particularly
beautiful upright form.
Its soft pink flowers are
star-shaped and
arranged in clusters
close to the branches.

Ptelea trifoliata
Hop tree
Rutaceae

The untoothed leaves are divided into 3 leaflets, each about 4 in. (10cm) long. Like many plants of the family Rutaceae *they release an aromatic vapor when crushed.*

Although not often seen in gardens, this small shrubby tree is easy to grow and has a modest beauty that combines well with more flamboyant plants. It forms a spreading, usually multi-stemmed plant that rarely exceeds 26 ft. (8m) in height, with a similar width. Its leaves are divided into 3 dark glossy leaflets and are aromatic when crushed. The flowers are small and yellow-green and arranged in dense heads. They appear in early summer and, although not visually conspicuous, are among the most attractively fragrant of any temperate garden plant. The fruits that follow are rather like those of elm, each consisting of a pair of seeds enclosed by a broad circular wing. They are borne in tight clusters and gradually turn from green to brown.

As well as being very hardy, the hop tree has easily provided requirements, with any well-drained, fertile soil being suitable. Although not shapely or colorful enough to be a natural specimen plant, its interesting foliage and delicate flowers make it a valuable and unusual addition for the larger shrub bed.

The bark is dark gray and, though smooth when young, becomes increasingly craggy and fissured with age.

Other trees

The only commonly available cultivar is 'Aurea,' a selection whose leaves are a striking yellow when young, gradually fading to lime-green. It is particularly effective planted in combination with other distinctively colored plants such as purple-leaved *Cotinus,* or dark green conifers.

The elm-like fruits (right) are composed of a pair of seeds surrounded by a flat green wing. They are borne in clusters and are more conspicuous than the flowers from which they arise.

factfinder

height	up to about 26 ft. (8m)
hardiness	zone 3
aspect	full sun to light shade
soil type	fertile, well drained
soil pH	acid to moderately alkaline
country of origin	eastern North America, Mexico

P. Trifoliata (right) often becomes a spreading multi-stemmed tree with a dense crown of dark foliage. It may be trained to a more upright form by formative pruning and tolerates hard pruning to reduce spread.

Even young trees produce abundant blossom and quickly become a valuable part of the garden landscape.

Pyrus calleryana
Callery pear

Rosaceae

The wild form of callery pear is a medium-sized tree from China and Korea, and is rarely seen in cultivation. It is best known for its grafted cultivars whose ornamental and cultural attributes have made them popular city trees. Their white flowers are produced in early spring, and give rise to small brown fruits that may be round or slightly pear-shaped. The leaves are oval and glossy and, in some selections, provide excellent fall color. All forms are known for their tolerance of dry or compacted soils and polluted air. They may be grown in a variety of soil types or pH, but do not thrive in heavy shade. Fireblight is the most significant problem, and in areas of greater prevalence of the disease cultivars should be chosen for their resistance.

Other trees

Probably the most widely planted selection is 'Bradford,' a small to medium-sized tree that can reach 50 ft. (15m) in height with a broadly

factfinder	
height	up to about 50 ft. (15m), but many smaller cultivars
hardiness	zone 5
aspect	full sun
soil type	fertile, well drained
soil pH	very tolerant
country of origin	China, Korea (species)
observation	some cultivars susceptible to fireblight

The fruit (below) are up to 1 in. (2.5cm) across and ripen to russet. They may be round or pear-shaped with a soft fleshy consistency.

conical crown. It is renowned for its flower abundance and fine fall color, its leaves turning bright orange and red. It is one of the most resistant cultivars to fireblight, but has a reputation for becoming brittle and liable to branch drop in old age. 'Chanticleer' is another North American selection with a narrow columnar shape that has made it a very popular street tree. It grows to a height of about 33 ft. (10m) and is therefore more suitable than 'Bradford' for small gardens. It also has good fireblight resistance.

The white flowers are 5-petaled and form clusters among the new leaves in early spring. The leaves are glossy and in some years provide good fall color.

Pyrus calleryana 'Chanticleer' (right) is one of the most widely planted cultivars. It is suitable for confined spaces and small gardens.

Pyrus salicifolia 'Pendula'
Weeping willow-leaved pear

Rosaceae

Unusually for a pear, the leaves are narrow and willow-like. They are covered in a fine coat of pale hairs that gives them an overall blue-gray appearance.

Not at all pear-like in appearance, this small tree has a graceful weeping form accentuated by its narrow willow-like leaves. It is ideal for smaller gardens, rarely exceeding 26 ft. (8m) in height, with a compact, rounded shape. Its flowers appear at about the same time as the new leaves and are followed by small green pears. However, neither rivals the beauty of the foliage, particularly early in the year when the young leaves are covered in a fine blue-gray pubescence. This is an extremely popular tree in Europe and would be more so in North America were it not for its susceptibility to fireblight. It is unsuitable for planting in areas of greater prevalence of the disease, especially in the south. Where this is less of a problem, its tolerance of a wide range of soil types and pH make it well worth considering, particularly for its unusual combination of shape, texture, and color.

factfinder

height	up to about 26 ft. (8m)
hardiness	zone 4
aspect	full sun
soil type	fertile, well drained
soil pH	moderately acid to alkaline
country of origin	western Asia, southeastern Europe (species)
observation	susceptible to fireblight

The fruit (above) are hard green pears about 1 in. (2.5cm) long and with a short stalk.

The flowers (above) are white with red anthers and, although not the tree's greatest asset, provide additional spring interest. They give rise to small green pears.

As a specimen tree (right) the combination of shape, texture, and color makes a strong impression. An open position in full sun is best to allow full development and allow the weeping branches to cascade right to the ground. The species Pyrus salicifolia (left) is a small tree with a more upright form than 'Pendula.' It shares the cultivar's fine foliage and makes an attractive tree where more space is available.

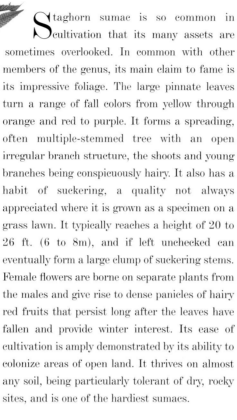

Rhus typhina
Staghorn sumac
Anacardiaceae

Staghorn sumac is so common in cultivation that its many assets are sometimes overlooked. In common with other members of the genus, its main claim to fame is its impressive foliage. The large pinnate leaves turn a range of fall colors from yellow through orange and red to purple. It forms a spreading, often multiple-stemmed tree with an open irregular branch structure, the shoots and young branches being conspicuously hairy. It also has a habit of suckering, a quality not always appreciated where it is grown as a specimen on a grass lawn. It typically reaches a height of 20 to 26 ft. (6 to 8m), and if left unchecked can eventually form a large clump of suckering stems. Female flowers are borne on separate plants from the males and give rise to dense panicles of hairy red fruits that persist long after the leaves have fallen and provide winter interest. Its ease of cultivation is amply demonstrated by its ability to colonize areas of open land. It thrives on almost any soil, being particularly tolerant of dry, rocky sites, and is one of the hardiest sumacs.

The dark red fruits (above) are borne in dense hairy clusters from early fall.

The new leaves of R. trichocarpa (below) are colored bright yellow-green, sometimes with a pink or purple tinge.

Throughout the winter months the fruits of R. typhina (below) remain on the bare branches.

factfinder

height	up to about 33 ft. (10m), but typically 20-26 ft. (6-8m)
hardiness	zone 3 (*R. trichocarpa* 8, *R. glabra* 2)
aspect	full sun to light shade
soil type	very tolerant
soil pH	very tolerant
country of origin	eastern North America

Other trees

The female cultivar 'Dissecta' ('Laciniata') has deeply divided leaflets that give the foliage a finely textured, fern-like appearance. They turn bright yellow and orange in fall. A number of other *Rhus* species are commonly cultivated. *R. trichocarpa* is a small tree from eastern Asia whose leaves are colored pink when young. In contrast to *R. typhina*, its fruits are yellow and held drooping rather than upright, and it is much less hardy (zone 8). *R. glabra* is a very hardy North American species whose main difference from *R. typhina* is its non-hairy stems. It too has a cut-leaved cultivar named 'Laciniata.'

The leaves of R. trichocarpa (above) turn glorious tones of marmalade orange in fall.

The bark of R. typhina (left) is gray and smooth with a speckling of narrow lenticels.

Robinia pseudoacacia
Black locust, false acacia
Leguminosae

The fruit are brown-red seed pods up to 4 in. (10cm) long. They often hang from the branches in great abundance.

The leaves are pinnate, with up to 21 oval leaflets (below). The thorned stems (below right) may be considered either as an attractive feature, or a problem if growing where children play.

The wild form of black locust is a large, rough-barked tree that can spread rapidly by seeds and suckers. It is frequently seen in large parks and arboreta, but is not suitable for most domestic gardens. Fortunately it has given rise to a number of more modestly sized cultivars that offer a variety of interesting features. All share the species' delicately shaped pinnate leaves and dark, attractively furrowed bark. However, the fragrant pea-like flowers are less abundant on some, and others have been selected for their absence of spines. They are tolerant of fairly poor soils, particularly those liable to drought, and need a sunny situation to perform well. In some areas of the USA outside its natural range the species is considered a pest due to its ability to spread, and should not be planted.

Other trees

The best known and widely grown cultivar is 'Frisia.' Its brilliant golden-yellow leaves stand out even at a distance and are particularly effective when combined with a background of dark green or purple foliaged plants. It commonly grows to about 33 ft. (10m), and occasionally a little more. Where a smaller plant is needed it may be regularly hard-pruned to produce a multiple-stemmed shrub with masses of foliage. For a

The bark is gray or pale brown, becoming increasingly fissured with scaly ridges.

completely different effect 'Tortuosa' is a similar sized but slower growing tree with contorted branches that are at their most dramatic in winter. The so-called mop-headed acacia, 'Umbraculifera' is, as the name suggests, a small round-topped tree that reaches a height of about 20 ft. (6m). 'Bessoniana' is a popular street tree due to its lack of spines and compact crown.

factfinder

height	up to about 33 ft. (10m)
hardiness	zone 3
aspect	full sun
soil type	very tolerant
soil pH	very tolerant
country of origin	eastern USA
observation	may be invasive in some areas

Wherever it is planted, R. pseudoacacia *has a strong visual impact (right). Used sparingly, it can provide a focal point in the garden and combines well with artificial features.*

Regular pruning of pollards provides a renewable supply of bright young stems. Older bark soon fades to a green-brown color if left unpruned.

Salix alba 'Britzensis' ('Chermesina')

Scarlet willow

Salicaceae

factfinder	
height	up to about 50 ft. (15m), but best regularly pruned
hardiness	zone 2
aspect	full sun
soil type	any fertile, moist
soil pH	moderately alkaline to acid
country of origin	Europe, western Asia (species)

White willow, *Salix alba*, is a large, vigorous tree that, given the chance, will overwhelm all but the largest of gardens. Fortunately many of its undoubted assets are shared by its various smaller cultivars including this one, whose name is derived from its dazzling flame-red stems. If left unchecked it can grow to a height of 50 ft. (15m), but to really make the most of its color it should be pruned regularly every 2 or 3 years to encourage a fresh growth of bright young stems. The height of cutting is unimportant, but is usually done either close to the ground (coppicing) or at about chest height (pollarding), and is best started when the tree is still fairly young. Pruning should be carried out in early spring, after the stems have provided valuable color during the drab winter days but well before leaf flush. In addition, the "harvest" of cut stems can be tied in bunches for indoor display.

Although capable of living in waterlogged conditions, it is also quite at home in better-drained soils provided they are not very alkaline or liable to drying. It is extremely hardy, preferring an open location in full sunlight. It may be grown as an individual specimen but is particularly impressive in a group, either unmixed or in combination with contrastingly colored willows or dogwoods.

To encourage new stems, plants may be cut to just above ground level. S. alba *var.* vitellina *(above) looks good grown in small groups and pruned like this every other year.*

The glossy young bark of S. alba var. vitellina *(right) is golden, and looks particularly dramatic combined with other stem colors.*

Other trees

Another well-known form of the species grown for its stem color is the golden willow, *S. alba* var. *vitellina.* As its name suggests, the young stems are golden yellow and, like 'Britzensis,' are best encouraged by regular pruning. Var. *sericea* is a medium-sized tree reaching a height of about 50 ft. (15m), which is grown primarily for its attractive silver-blue leaves.

Trees pollarded at about
chest height (above)
make a striking sight
and are suitable for
a small garden. Small
groups like this one
make an even
greater impact.

The young shoots of
'Britzensis' (left) grow
rapidly from cut stumps
or pollards, and look
especially spectacular
illuminated by
winter sunlight.

The male catkins of S. daphnoides 'Aglaia' (right) are produced in early spring. They start fluffy gray and gradually turn bright yellow as the anthers mature.

Salix daphnoides
Violet willow

Salicaceae

Despite its vigorous early growth, violet willow seldom grows to much more than 33 ft. (10m) in height, and is one of the very best species for small gardens. If allowed to develop naturally, its ascending branches form a broad conical crown that tends to spread with age. Its deep purple shoots are covered in a pale bloom and are particularly conspicuous during the leafless winter months. Like many other species of willow, it responds well to hard pruning every year or two by throwing out a new crop of young shoots. This should be carried out in mid-spring, before the emergence of leaves but after male plants have had the opportunity to display their large yellow catkins. The narrow leaves are glossy green above with blue-tinged undersides and are a feature in themselves.

This is a very hardy species that thrives in exposed situations and poor, wet soils. It is less successful in dry or shallow alkaline conditions and particularly dislikes shade. It looks good planted in a group with a dark evergreen background to emphasize the texture and color of the shoots.

Other trees

The cultivar 'Aglaia' is a male clone selected for its impressive bright yellow catkins. Its shoots vary from the species in that they are unbloomed and bright red in winter.

The European goat willow, *Salix caprea*, has given rise to a number of attractive cultivars that fit comfortably into a small garden. The weeping forms 'Kilmarnock' and 'Weeping Sally' are male and female respectively and make ornate, umbrella-shaped trees that typically grow to about 6 ft. (2m). Although often referred to collectively as 'Pendula,' the males can be distinguished easily by their silver-gray woolly catkins.

factfinder	
height	about 33 ft. (10m), but may be regularly pruned
hardiness	zone 2 (*S. caprea* 4)
aspect	full sun
soil type	all but shallow and dry
soil pH	acid to moderately alkaline
country of origin	northern Europe to Himalayas

Regular hard pruning (below) maintains a tree at a manageable size, and provides a ready supply of colorful young stems. Pruning may be done in a number of ways to produce whatever size and shape of plant is wanted.

Purple-gray stems (above and above right) combine well with groups of other stem-color plants like willows and dogwoods. Concentrating plants like this within easy view from a window provides welcome winter color.

The leaves (above) are up to 4 in. (10cm) long, and curled. The undersides are blue-green when young, contrasting with brighter green upper sides. The young shoots are glossy purple-brown or yellow.

Salix matsudana 'Tortuosa'
Dragon's claw willow

Salicaceae

This is a tree for those looking for something to catch the eye. It is one of the most distinctive willows, grown for its unusual stems and attractive foliage. It has an upright habit with lower branches often drooping to the ground, giving it a graceful appearance. In ideal conditions it may reach a height of 40 ft. (12m), though usually less. The leaves are long and slender and slightly contorted with a conspicuous contrast between upper and lower surfaces. The shoots are attractive for their coloration as well as growth habit. The full effect of the contorted branches can be best appreciated in winter when unobscured by leaves. Like other willows it can be heavily pruned from time to time at waist height

or above to promote vigorous new growth. It does best in a sunny location and moist soil. Some authorities have reclassified this species, and it may now be sold as *S. babylonica* var. *pekinensis* 'Tortuosa.'

factfinder	
height	up to about 40 ft. (12m)
hardiness	zone 6
aspect	full sun
soil type	moist
soil pH	moderately acid or alkaline
country of origin	China

Most trees develop a narrow upright shape (left) with a rounded top. Where desirable, low pruning may be carried out to expose a clear trunk.

The fruit are glossy red berries borne in hanging clusters through late summer and fall.

Sorbus aria
Whitebeam

Rosaceae

A popular tree in its native Europe, whitebeam is a far less common sight in North American gardens where the mountain ash, *Sorbus aucuparia*, tends to be favored. However, given suitable conditions it is a tough tree with a number of attributes that make it worth considering. It commonly grows to a height of about 40 ft. (12m), with a single clear trunk and dense round crown. Its large simple leaves have pale downy undersides and are a striking sight when ruffled by a light breeze. The creamy white flowers are borne in clusters in late spring and eventually give rise to bunches of bright red berries that provide rich pickings for birds. They combine with the gold and amber tones of the turning leaves to make this a good tree for fall color.

factfinder

height	up to about 40 ft. (12m)
hardiness	zone 3
aspect	full sun to light shade
soil type	moist, well drained
soil pH	very tolerant
country of origin	Europe
observation	susceptible to fireblight

It is not a species for dry climates, especially those with hot summers, and use in unsuitable conditions has contributed to its relative unpopularity. It does, however, thrive in cooler maritime climates and tolerates shallow lime soils and coastal exposure. It is very susceptible to fireblight, and in areas where the disease is prevalent other more resistant species should be chosen.

Other trees

Similar in stature and general appearance to the species is the cultivar 'Lutescens.' Its young leaves are only distinguishable in spring when their upper sides are covered in a pale creamy down. The leaves of 'Chrysophylla' remain yellow-green right through the summer before turning brighter yellow in fall. The Swedish whitebeam, *S. intermedia*, is a similar but slightly larger species with lobed leaves. It has the great advantage of being resistant to fireblight.

The young leaves of 'Chrysophylla' (above) are yellow-green, turning to bright butter yellow in the fall. They contrast well with a background of darker colors.

Similar in shape and size to the species, 'Lutescens' (left) can be distinguished in the spring when the upper surfaces of its leaves are covered in a fine creamy white pubescence.

A typically shaped tree (right) has a short single trunk and broad round crown. Its regular outline lends itself well to being grown either as a single specimen or in avenues or other formal groups.

The leaves (above) are pinnate with between 11 and 19 toothed leaflets. In some years they display excellent fall colors of red and orange.

Sorbus aucuparia
European mountain ash, rowan

Rosaceae

This is by far the most commonly cultivated *Sorbus* both in its native Europe and adopted homeland of North America. Its attributes are many, and plant breeders have exploited its variability to produce a range of attractive garden forms. The species sometimes develops the stature of a medium-sized tree up to 50 ft. (15m) tall with a broad rounded crown, and for domestic gardens one of the smaller cultivars is often a better choice. It owes much of its popularity to the brilliance and abundance of its red to orange fruit that greatly upstage the clusters of white flowers from which they develop. They hang in heavy clusters and, although edible for humans, prove even more so for birds. The compound leaves have a delicate beauty that is emphasized in the fall when they put on a fine display of color from yellow and orange through red to purple.

It prefers a moist but well-drained soil from neutral to acid. In the wild it often grows as an understorey tree beneath larger trees, a characteristic that can be useful in shady gardens. It also makes a fine specimen in a lawn or other

factfinder	
height	up to about 50 ft. (15m), but some cultivars less
hardiness	zone 3
aspect	full sun to moderate shade
soil type	moist, well drained
soil pH	neutral to acid
country of origin	Europe, western Asia
observation	susceptible to fireblight

prominent position. Though less susceptible to fireblight than *S. aria*, it is by no means immune, and the more resistant cultivars should be chosen in areas where the disease is prevalent.

Other trees

Where space is a limiting factor 'Fastigiata' provides a slow growing and narrow tree that rarely exceeds 20 ft. (6m) in height. Both its leaves and fruit are larger than those of the species. 'Beissneri' is similar in size to the species but differs in shape, its crown of strongly ascending branches giving it a quite distinctive appearance. The bark of its trunk and large branches is an attractive orange-brown, and the young shoots are coral-red.

The fruit are borne in dense bunches from late summer and provide food for birds. The cultivar 'Streetwise' is renowned for its abundant bright orange-red fruit. The bark (far right) is smooth and gray.

The neat rounded shape of S. aucuparia *(right) is one of the attributes that make it particularly suitable for small gardens. The flowers are produced in late spring.*

Sorbus vilmorinii
Vilmorin mountain ash

Rosaceae

Though superficially similar to its far more common relative *S. aucuparia,* this Chinese species is quite distinct and well worth considering for something a little unusual. It is an ideal tree for small gardens, rarely exceeding a height of 20 ft. (6m) with a broad, open crown of slender branches. Its compound leaves are composed of numerous small leaflets, giving them a delicate ferny appearance. The fruits develop from creamy white flowers and, though initially deep red, gradually pass through shades of pink to white as they ripen. They are borne in hanging clusters and often persist right through fall to early winter, providing a beautiful contrast with the deep red and purple of the turning leaves. The cultural requirements are similar to those of *S. aucuparia:* a moist but well-drained neutral to acid soil in a sunny or lightly shaded situation.

The delicate leaves (above) are composed of up to 25 leaflets, each about 1 in. (2.5cm) long. They are gray-green in color, turning in fall to deep red and purple.

factfinder	
height	up to about 20 ft. (6m)
hardiness	zone 3
aspect	full sun to partial shade
soil type	moist, well drained
soil pH	neutral to acid
country of origin	western China

Other trees

There are a number of other pale-fruited species from China. *S. hupehensis* has pink-tinged white berries that often last long into the winter due to their apparent lack of appeal to birds. It grows to a height of about 33 ft. (10m) and is recognizable by its silvery gray-green leaves. *S. cashmeriana* is a little smaller at about 26 ft. (8m), and has large white fruit suspended from red stalks. It is unusual in having pink flowers.

The fruit of S. hupehensis (left) are often produced in great abundance and remain on the tree long after the leaves have been shed.

The berries are small spheres hanging in slender-staked bunches. They start dark red and gradually turn through pink to white.

The leaves are trifoliate, with narrow pointed leaflets.

Staphylea holocarpa
Bladder nut

Staphyleaceae

Despite its absence from many nursery catalogs, bladder nut makes an attractive and versatile small tree for the garden. Its habit is variable and often more spreading shrub than tree-like. However, it can occasionally reach 33 ft. (10m) in height, with a number of stems and a broad spread. Its leaves are trifoliate and emerge at about the same time as the loose panicles of white flowers in spring. These are followed by conspicuous bladder-like fruits that give the plant its name, and which persist long into the fall. It is a very adaptable tree, able to grow in any fertile soil in either full sun or partial shade. Planted in a large shrub border it provides attractive foliage along with the spring and fall interest of its flowers and fruit.

factfinder

height	up to about 33 ft. (10m), but usually less
hardiness	zone 6
aspect	full sun to partial shade
soil type	any fertile, well drained
soil pH	moderately acid or alkaline
country of origin	central China

Other trees

The cultivar 'Rosea' has pink flowers and is as common in cultivation as the species. Its leaves, though eventually shiny green, open an attractive bronze color. A number of other bladder nuts are in cultivation. Most are shrubs including *S. colchica*, a Caucasian species whose white flowers are held in long erect panicles and give rise to fruit capsules up to 4 in. (10cm) long.

The white flowers (above) open from rose-colored buds in late spring, and are borne in short drooping panicles. The popular cultivar 'Rosea' (right) has pink-tinged flowers.

The showy flowers have 5 white petals and appear from mid- to late summer.

Stewartia sinensis
Chinese Stewartia

Theaceae

Less well known than the Japanese Stewartia, *S. pseudocamellia,* this species shares many of its relative's attributes in a more compact form, better suited to the small garden. It grows to a height of about 20 ft. (6m), with a broad crown that tends to divide low into a number of main stems. The flaking, patterned bark is one of its main attributes and elevates it to the ranks of a tree for all seasons. It varies in color considerably from one individual to the next and even within one tree, ranging from rusty brown through gray to pale yellow. The fragrant flowers are creamy white open cups that, although individually short-lived, flower in succession for about a month in mid- to late summer. Fall leaf color is unreliable, but in good years ranges from bright red to orange.

Although one of the hardier *Stewartias,* it prefers a sheltered location and does well in the shade of larger trees. It requires a moist and fertile acid soil and particular care should be taken in choosing a location as it resents movement when of any size. Pruning is unnecessary and is unlikely to succeed in achieving a dominant central trunk.

factfinder

height	up to about 20 ft. (6m)
hardiness	zone 5 (*S. pseudocamellia* 5, *S. serrata* 6)
aspect	partial shade and shelter
soil type	moist, fertile
soil pH	acid
country of origin	central China

Other trees

There are a number of other species of *Stewartia* with similar attributes, and choice should be based on size, ease of cultivation, and availability. *S. pseudocamellia* is probably the best for general use but is rather too large for the smallest gardens with a height of over 50 ft. (15m) in suitable conditions. Its multi-colored flaking bark and fine fall colors of yellow and red are perhaps the most dramatic of all the species. *S. serrata* is a small Japanese tree with a height of about 33 ft. (10m). Its flowers appear earlier than other species in early summer and have petals stained red at their bases. Virginia Stewartia, *S. malacodendron,* is a less hardy species (zone 7) with a similar stature and requirements to *S. sinensis.*

The bark (below) varies in color from silver-gray to orange, often flaking attractively.

S. sinensis (right) develops into a small tree, often branching low to form a broad crown of attractively barked branches.

142

The pale gray fruit of S. japonica are delicate globes suspended by long stalks.

Styrax japonica
Japanese snowbell

Styracaceae

This is the most widely grown snowbell, being relatively easy to cultivate, a reliable flower producer, and readily obtainable. It is also a suitably sized tree for the small garden, only occasionally exceeding 33 ft. (10m) in height. Its slender branches spread broadly and form a framework from which the early summer flowers hang in great abundance. The fruits are often overlooked due to their small size but are delicate, egg-shaped orbs that are well worth close examination. The smooth gray bark provides an interesting contrast with the dark foliage.

It requires a moist, acid soil in full sun or light shade and, particularly in colder or exposed areas, benefits from some shelter. Because of the arrangement of its pendulous flowers beneath the densely foliaged branches, it is often planted in an elevated position on a bank or raised bed to allow viewing from below. In a small garden where its spread cannot be accommodated easily it may be pruned while young to encourage a more upright form with a central leader. However, this is likely to be only partially successful, and ideally it should be allowed to develop naturally.

factfinder

height	up to about 33 ft. (10m)
hardiness	zone 4 (*S. obassia* 5)
aspect	full sun to partial shade
soil type	moist, well drained
soil pH	acid
country of origin	Japan, Korea

Other trees

'Pink Chimes' is the best-known cultivar of the species. It produces an abundance of pink flowers even on young plants. *S. obassia* forms a large shrub or small tree with a height of up to 40 ft. (12m) and an upright, often multiple-stemmed, crown. Its highly fragrant flowers are white with yellow anthers and are held in horizontal racemes up to 6 in. (15cm) long. A notable feature is the leaves, which are almost round with a delicate drip tip, and color yellow in fall.

The flowers of S. obassia are white with yellow anthers (above). Each is about 1 in. (2.5cm) long and arranged in horizontal racemes in mid-summer.

S. japonica (right) forms a densely foliaged tree with low branches sweeping to the ground.

The leaves of S. obassia (left) are almost circular, with a fine tip. The blue-gray undersides are covered in fine hair and contrast with the darker tops. In fall they turn yellow.

The creamy white flowers are borne in large frothy panicles.

Syringa reticulata
Japanese tree lilac

Oleaceae

One of the few lilacs that can truly be described as a tree, this species may reach a height of 26 ft. (8m) with almost as great a spread. Its eventual form is variable, and dependent to some extent on early pruning. Trees with a clear trunk best display the shiny chestnut-brown bark whose horizontal lenticels give it a cherry-like appearance. Its flowers are white and borne in long panicles up to 12 in. (30cm) long in late spring/early summer. Their fragrance is less pleasant than many other lilacs, being more like that of privet.

In common with other lilacs, it is a useful plant for dry sites, particularly those with shallow alkaline soils. However, on particularly poor soils it benefits from occasional mulching or feeding. It flowers best in full sunshine, though light shade is tolerated and may help reduce its susceptibility to damage by late frosts. It is very resistant to the problems of mildew and scale suffered by other lilacs. Where a tree form is wanted, training should be carried out from a young age by phased pruning of side branches and secondary stems.

factfinder

height	up to about 26 ft. (8m)
hardiness	zone 3
aspect	full sun
soil type	well drained
soil pH	moderately acid to alkaline
country of origin	Japan

Other trees

The species has given rise to a number of cultivars that have been selected for their consistent flower production or form. 'Ivory Silk' is a little smaller than the species with a height of up to 20 ft. (6m) and a more compact tree form. It also has a reputation for prolific flowering. 'Summer Snow' has a broad rounded crown and superior glossy green leaves.

S. reticulata (right) often forms a broad multiple-stemmed tree with a dense cover of dark foliage. In late spring or early summer the crown becomes almost completely covered in the flowers.

The dark green leaves (left) are up to 5 in. (13cm) long, and often give good fall color.

The typical foliage is composed of ranks of soft pointed needles each about 1 in. (2.5cm) long. The numerous cultivars differ widely in the color, arrangement, and texture of their foliage and provide garden designers with a great range of possibilities.

Taxus baccata
English yew

Taxaceae

In the wild and in cultivation, English yew can grow to a great size and live to an immense age. It has a multitude of functional and ornamental uses, from hedging and screening to individual specimen or avenue planting. For smaller-scale landscapes and domestic gardens it has given rise to numerous more compact cultivars that share the species' attributes of adaptability and resilience. Although variously colored and displaying a range of textural effects, their lush evergreen foliage is the main feature of interest. Female plants also produce attractive fruits that, despite containing poisonous seeds, prove very popular with birds. The bark becomes furrowed and twisted with age and lends the tree great character.

It thrives in almost any kind of soil from moist alkaline clays to dry acid sands, with only poorly drained sites being out of bounds. Though generally tolerant to exposure, cold winds can cause browning of the foliage. One of the tree's most useful attributes is its ability to withstand even extreme pruning, and if regularly trimmed it can be encouraged to adopt almost any shape, from formal geometric to amorphous lump.

The bark develops an interesting landscape of curves and hollows. Older trees become flaky and display a range of pinks and rusty browns.

factfinder

height	up about to 65 ft. (20m); cultivars variable, down to dwarfs
hardiness	zone 5
aspect	full sun to heavy shade
soil type	any except poorly drained
soil pH	any
country of origin	Europe, northern Africa, western Asia
observation	toxic seeds and foliage

T. baccata 'Standishii' (below and right) combines unusual shape with bright foliage and colorful fruit. Its golden foliage is particularly intense during the winter months.

Other trees

The list of cultivars is very long, and the following are just a few of those most suitable for small gardens. The Irish yew, 'Fastigiata,' is a popular female selection that forms a column of dark green foliage with leaves arranged radially around the shoots. It starts fairly narrow but broadens out with age and may reach a height of 26 ft. (8m). Its shape lends itself to formal situations and it is often trimmed to give a flat top. 'Standishii' is another female with a similar shape, but is slow growing and has golden leaves. 'Adpressa Variegata' is a male that grows to about 6 ft. (2m). The young foliage is golden, gradually changing to green with yellow margins.

Tetradium daniellii
Korean evodia

Rutaceae

This is an uncommon tree in both North American and European gardens. Its charms, though understated, are numerous, and it is well worth considering for larger gardens where something out of the ordinary is wanted. It varies in size, typically growing to a height of 26 to 33 ft. (8 to 10m), with a similar spread. Its pinnate leaves have up to 11 leaflets with dark glossy upper surfaces. The flowers are creamy white and, though individually small, are arranged in large flattened heads that can cover the crown of a mature tree. They are borne in late summer when their strong scent proves a popular lure to bees. They give rise to dense bunches of small purple-red fruits that ripen to black before splitting open to reveal the seeds.

It is an adaptable tree, not fussy about either soil type or pH, and has sufficient ornamental value to make a good specimen. Although not generally available in the commercial plant trade, it can be obtained from more specialist nurseries, often under its former name of *Euodia daniellii*.

Other trees

Of the 9 species of *Tetradium* this is the only one commonly cultivated in Europe and North America. Its close relative, the Amur cork tree, *Phellodendron amurense*, is a more widely planted species that grows to a similar stature. It is similar in many respects but easily distinguished by its rough corky bark, from which it gets its name. Its inconspicuous flowers are yellowy green, and its leaves turn yellow in fall.

The pinnate leaves are about 10 in. (25cm) long with up to 11 untoothed leaflets. When crushed they release a strongly scented vapor.

The fruit are rusty red or purple, with small "beaks" at their tops. They gradually turn black before opening.

T. daniellii usually develops a neat symmetrical outline (right and far right) with a single trunk and round open crown.

factfinder	
height	typically 26–33 ft. (8–10m), but up to about 50 ft. (15m)
hardiness	zone 4
aspect	full sun to partial shade
soil type	fertile, well drained
soil pH	moderately acid or alkaline
country of origin	China, Korea

The strongly scented flowers (above left) are arranged in branched heads. The males have bright yellow anthers and are borne separately from the females. The bark (above right) is smooth and dark gray, often with attractive specks of pale brown or gray.

Tilia mongolica
Mongolian lime

Tiliaceae

Although unreliable as a fall colorer, in good years the leaves provide a beautiful display of clear yellow tones.

O ne of the few limes suitable for a small garden, this Asian beauty is far from typical of the genus. It rarely grows taller than about 33 ft. (10m) with a rounded crown, compact enough to fit into a moderately confined space. Its leaves are carried on conspicuously red stalks and are sharply and irregularly toothed, more like a large-leaved hawthorn than a lime. They often have a reddish tinge when young, later becoming dark glossy green, and end the year by turning a beautiful golden yellow. The flowers appear in summer and are more notable for their fragrance than their looks. In the wild, the species inhabits mountain slopes at high altitude and is well equipped to survive all but the very coldest of climates.

The leaves (below) are rounded with ragged, irregular teeth, and a long tip. They gradually darken through the summer before coloring in fall.

It prefers a reasonably fertile soil with a moderate pH either side of neutral. It dislikes drought, and benefits from watering during dry spells and mulching to preserve soil moisture. In common with most other limes, gradual but repeated pruning while young will encourage the development of a central leader and avoid weak forking. The species is considered less liable to

factfinder	
height	up to about 33 ft. (10m)
hardiness	zone 3
aspect	full sun to moderate shade
soil type	fertile, moist but well drained
soil pH	moderately acid or alkaline
country of origin	Mongolia, northern China, eastern Russia

aphid infestation and resultant honeydew drop than some other limes, making it suitable for planting near driveways. It is an ideal specimen tree for small gardens and, though somewhat unusual, should be obtainable without much difficulty through more specialized nurseries.

Other trees

T. mongolica 'Harvest Gold' is a fairly recently named selection of the hybrid between Mongolian lime and European small-leaved lime, *T. cordata*. It grows to a height of about 40 ft. (12m), and has less deeply toothed leaves and bark that flakes with age.

The flowers (above) are pale yellow and hang in small clusters in mid-summer. Their fragrance draws more attention than their looks.

The bark (above) is pale gray or brown with a smooth but textured surface. T. mongolica (right) develops an upright tree, usually with a single dominant trunk, and is adaptable enough to grow in the light shade of larger trees.

The fan-shaped leaves (above) are up to 4 ft. (1.2m) across, bright green above with paler blue-green undersides. Their large size makes them particularly useful for providing contrast of scale.

Trachycarpus fortunei
Windmill palm, Chusan palm

Palmae

One of the few palms hardy enough to grow in cool climates, windmill palm lends a tropical feel to any garden mild enough to accommodate it. Its main asset is the huge, fan-shaped leaves, providing a highly unusual combination of shape and pattern. They arise from the fibrous trunk via a thick, toothed stalk, and last for many years. It may eventually reach a height of up to 33 ft. (10m), never spreading further than the length of the leaves. The tiny flowers are arranged in dense clusters, borne on thick stalks in early summer. Although reasonably hardy, it benefits greatly from shelter, with the leaves in particular being very susceptible to wind damage.

It will grow in a variety of well-drained soils but does not thrive in anything more than light shade. The only pruning necessary is an occasional tidying-up removal of dead leaves to leave a short stub on the trunk. Its unique shape makes this a natural specimen plant, creating a strong visual impression among more conventional temperate plants. It should be used sparingly to avoid "dilution" of its very novel appearance.

factfinder

height	up to about 33 ft. (10m)
hardiness	zone 7 (C. australis 8)
aspect	full sun (best) to light shade
soil type	fertile, well drained
soil pH	moderately acid or alkaline
country of origin	China

Other trees

The giant dracena or cabbage palm, *Cordyline australis*, is a member of the agave family and, though unrelated to windmill palm, creates a similarly striking impression in cool temperate gardens. It grows to a similar height, usually with a single trunk and a number of thick, ascending branches, each ending in a crown of sharp, sword-like leaves. It is a native of New Zealand but has become a common sight in mild seaside areas, giving a "tropical island" feel even in winter.

The unusual foliage and overall shape make T. fortunei (right) an obvious choice for those seeking novelty. It benefits from shelter for its large vulnerable leaves.

The trunk is covered in a dense fibrous layer. Unlike most trees it is formed by the generation of new leaves and does not increase in girth once formed. Dead leaves should be pruned to leave a short stump (far right).

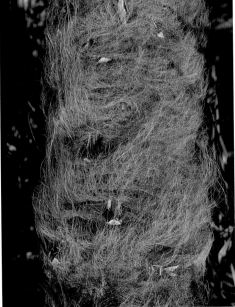

Ulmus glabra 'Camperdownii'
Camperdown elm

Ulmaceae.

First cultivated at Camperdown House in Scotland in 1850, this compact version of the European wych elm remains one of the best weeping trees for a small garden. It grows fairly slowly to form a semi-circular dome up to about 20 ft. (6m) tall. Its shape is created by "top-grafting" the weeping part of the tree onto a straight stem at a height of about 6 ft. (2m). During the summer, its sandpaper-rough leaves form a continuous canopy that cascades right down to the ground. In fall they turn yellow before dropping to reveal an impressive framework of bare, weeping branches. It should be planted where it can expand unhindered to its full, rounded extent, and is particularly suitable as a lone specimen on a lawn. Its gaunt winter branches look particularly dramatic against a dark evergreen background of yew or holly.

Like many weeping trees, it responds poorly to pruning and only trimming of the drooping branch ends and dead wooding should be carried out. It is a hardy tree that survives exposure, salt spray, and a variety of soil conditions. Although

The leaves are particularly attractive when young, the conspicuous veins giving them a pleated appearance. As they age the upper surfaces become increasingly rough to the touch.

Seen from beneath the sinuous branches are an attractive feature at all times of year.

The fruits are held in small clusters, each one consisting of a single seed surrounded by a circular wing. Although small, their pale yellow-green coloration makes them stand out against the surrounding new leaves.

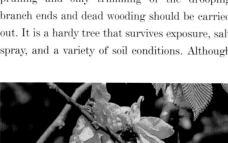

factfinder

height	up to about 20 ft. (6m)
hardiness	zone 4
aspect	full sun or light shade
soil type	very tolerant
soil pH	acid or alkaline
country of origin	Europe, northern and western Asia
observation	susceptible to Dutch elm disease

The tiny red flowers are arranged in round "pincushions" and appear before the leaves in early spring.

In late spring the new leaves and winged fruit coincide (right) and cover the skeleton of descending branches.

susceptible to Dutch elm disease, it is far more resistant than the species and often thrives even in areas where the disease is prevalent.

Other trees

The cultivar 'Pendula' ('Horizontalis') has a flat-topped shape and is often known as the table elm. Although rarely more than 26 ft. (8m) tall, its spread is often greater, making it less suitable for small gardens than 'Camperdownii.'

Tree selector

The following pages give a selection of trees notable for one of six desirable features. Each selection can then be further narrowed down by checking the tree's tolerances and other attractive features. This information will help you to arrive at the best trees for a particular situation. For example, if a tree is needed to provide winter interest in a garden with poorly drained soil, the relevant column of the "winter interest" page shows that a number of trees fit the bill including *Ilex aquifolium* and *Salix daphnoides* 'Aglaia.'

Clockwise from top left:
Aesculus pavia
Amelanchier lamarckii
Cercis canadensis
Crinodendron hookerianum
Embothrium coccineum
Laburnum x *watereri*
Lagerstroemia indica x
    fauriei
Magnolia stellata
Center:
Prunus x *subhirtella*

Attractive flowers

Flowers are one of the most conspicuous markers of the changing seasons in the garden. They come in all shapes and sizes, from the small and delicate racemes of snake-bark maples to the loud and showy cups and saucers of magnolias. Some trees—like *Amelanchier lamarckii*—provide a brief but dramatic flower display, while others such as *Ligustrum lucidum* are less intense, but longer lasting. Of particular value are species that flower very early or late, when few others are in bloom. It is important for the sake of variety to choose trees that will provide contrast and a sequence of flowering times to cover most of the year.

NAME/DESCRIPTION	tolerates heavy clay soils	tolerates alkaline soils	tolerates poorly drained soils	tolerates dry soils	tolerates salt spray	tolerates exposure	tolerates extreme cold	evergreen	compact size	attractive fruit or cones	foliage interest	fall colour	attractive bark	winter interest
Aesculus pavia Flowers bright crimson in early to mid-summer	●	●								●		●		
Amelanchier lamarckii 'Ballerina' Star-like flowers in early spring	●		●									●		
Aralia elata Flowers in frothy white panicles in late summer/early fall	●	●	●								●	●		
Cercis canadensis Pink pea-like flowers in spring arise directly from the stems		●		●							●	●		
Chionanthus virginicus Fragrant early summer flowers with long narrow petals		●							●			●		
Cornus kousa Creamy white flower bracts cover the branches in early summer										●		●		
Crataegus laevigata 'Paul's Scarlet' Deep pink double flowers in spring	●	●	●		●	●				●		●		
Crinodendron hookerianum Flowers like crimson lanterns in late spring								●	●					
Embothrium coccineum Narrow tubular blooms produced in early summer			●					●						
Eucryphia glutinosa Fragrant white flowers with pink-tipped stamens in late summer								s				●		
Halesia carolina Snowdrop-like flowers hang in clusters in spring			●								●			
Hoheria glabrata Sweetly scented flowers hang from arched branches in mid-summer		●		●					●					
Koelreuteria paniculata Panicles of yellow blooms form in mid- to late summer		●		●							●			
Laburnum x *watereri* 'Vossii' Dangling racemes of pea-like flowers bloom in early summer	●	●		●		●								
Lagerstroemia indica x *fauriei* Flowers on new growth in late summer or early fall				●								●	●	●
Ligustrum lucidum Panicles of fragrant white flowers in late summer and fall	●	●		●									●	
Magnolia stellata Dazzling white flowers emerge from woolly buds in early spring	●								●		●			
Malus hupehensis Pink flower buds give rise to clusters of long-stalked white flowers	●	●								●				
Prunus x *subhirtella* Small pale pink flowers produced before the leaves in early spring	●	●										●		
Styrax japonica Flowers hang in great abundance in early summer				●							●			

KEY

Sp *spring* ■ **Su** *summer* ■ **F** *fall* ■ **W** *winter*

s *semi evergreen*

Clockwise from top left:
Arbutus unedo
Ficus carica
Halesia carolina
Ilex aquifolium
Malus floribunda
Morus nigra
Ptelea trifoliata
Rhus typhina
Center:
Sorbus aucuparia

Attractive fruit or cones

Many trees have colorful fruit, usually ripening in late summer and fall and providing interest when few flowers are around. The berries of many trees provide food for birds, while others—such as *Crataegus* x *lavelli*—are less palatable and remain well into the winter. Conifer cones are often retained long after the seeds have been shed and provide all-year-round interest. A few species are known for the novelty of their fruit—the winged "helicopters" of the maples are a great favorite with children, while the lantern-like pods of *Koelreuteria paniculata* rival the flowers for beauty.

NAME/DESCRIPTION	tolerates heavy clay soils	tolerates alkaline soils	tolerates poorly drained soils	tolerates dry soils	tolerates salt spray	tolerates exposure	tolerates extreme cold	evergreen	compact size	attractive flowers (season)	foliage interest	fall color	attractive bark	winter interest
Acer japonicum Fruits hang in pairs and have red-tinged wings										Sp	•	•		
Arbutus unedo Red fruits arising from previous year's flowers ripen in fall	•		•	•			•			F	•		•	•
Cornus alternifolia Small purplish black fruits form in clusters by mid-summer										Su	•			
Crataegus x *lavelli* 'Carrieri' Orange-red fruits remain on the tree through the winter	•	•	•		•	•				Sp		•		•
Euonymus hamiltonianus Flamboyantly colored fruits ripen in late summer	•	•		•					•			•		
Ficus carica Fruits turn from green to purple-brown through the summer		•		•							•			
Halesia carolina Attractive green fruits have 4 "wings" running from top to bottom				•						Sp				
Ilex aquifolium Female cultivars produce bright berries that last into winter	•	•		•	•	•		•			•			•
Koelreuteria paniculata Large lantern-like fruits turn from bright green to brown		•		•						Su		•		
Magnolia x *soulangiana* Fruits held in knobbly clusters that ripen to pink	•			•						Sp				
Malus floribunda Miniature shiny yellow apples often tinged pink or red	•	•							•	Sp				
Morus nigra Raspberry-like fruits excellent eaten fresh or preserved		•										•	•	
Photinia villosa Shiny red berries ripen in early fall				•						Sp		•		
Pinus aristata Oval-shaped cones have scales that end in a bristle-like spine				•		•	•	•						•
Ptelea trifoliata Fruits consist of a pair of seeds enclosed by a broad circular wing	•								•	Su				
Rhus typhina Dense panicles of hairy red fruits persist long after the leaves	•	•		•							•	•		•
Sorbus aucuparia Brilliant red to orange fruit produced in great abundance	•	•								Sp		•		
Staphylea holocarpa Conspicuous bladder-like fruits persist long into the fall	•									Sp				
Taxus baccata 'Fastigiata' Female plants produce attractive fruits, very popular with birds	•	•		•	•		•	•			•		•	•
Tetradium danielli Dense bunches of small purple-red fruits ripen to black		•								Su		•		

KEY

Sp *spring* ■ **Su** *summer* ■ **F** *fall* ■ **W** *winter*

Clockwise from top left:
Acer palmatum
    'Atropurpureum'
Azara microphylla
Chamaecyparis obtusa
    'Nana Aurea'
Cryptomeria japonica
    'Elegans'
Eucalyptus gunnii
Ficus carica
Ilex opaca
Pyrus salicifolia
Center:
Trachycarpus fortunei

Foliage interest

All trees worthy of a place in the garden must contribute to the overall foliar landscape, but some species have a special role in providing highlights, either in the form of unusual color or dramatic shape. Used well and sparingly, these plants can "lift" an otherwise monotonous border or provide a focal point in an important view. Careful combination of plants with contrasting foliage can be used to great visual effect—the delicacy of *Azara microphylla* can be emphasized by growing it alongside larger-leaved species. Evergreen species often fulfill a dual role, accompanying deciduous trees during the summer and taking center stage in winter.

NAME/DESCRIPTION	tolerates heavy clay soils	tolerates alkaline soils	tolerates poorly drained soils	tolerates dry soils	tolerates salt spray	tolerates exposure	tolerates extreme cold	evergreen	compact size	attractive flowers (season)	attractive fruit or cones	fall color	attractive bark	winter interest
Acer palmatum 'Atropurpureum' Crimson leaves throughout the summer turning flame red in fall										Sp	•	•		
Acer pseudoplatanus 'Brilliantissimum' Lobed leaves open a vibrant shade of pink	•	•		•	•		•							
Alnus glutinosa 'Imperialis' Leaves cut into narrow lobes giving them a feather-like appearance	•		•	•										•
Aralia elata Enormous leaves give the plant an unusual fern-like appearance										Su/F	•	•		
Azara microphylla 'Variegata' Tiny leaves arranged to create large fan-like sprays								•		Sp				
Chamaecyparis obtusa 'Crisppii' Golden foliage arranged on elegant branches with drooping tips	•	•	•	•		•		•						•
Chamaecyparis pisifera 'Filifera' Thread-like foliage hangs from drooping branchlets	•	•	•	•	•	•		•						•
Cordyline australis Ascending branches end in a crown of sharp, sword-like leaves					•			•		Su				•
Cornus controversa 'Variegata' Creamy-white-margined leaves arranged on layered branches									•	Sp	•			
Cryptomeria japonica 'Elegans' Fine-textured juvenile foliage turns an impressive bronze color	•	•	•			•	•	•						•
Eucalyptus gunnii Attractive juvenile leaves are rounded and silver-blue	•	•	•	•				•					•	•
Ficus carica Glossy leaves are fleshy and lobed and turn yellow in fall		•		•								•		
Ilex opaca Spiny leaves with matte green surfaces provide good winter cover			•		•		•	•						•
Magnolia grandiflora 'Little Gem' Leaves are glossy above and felted rusty-brown underneath	•	•						•	•	Su/F	•			
Pyrus salicifolia 'Pendula' Young leaves covered in a fine blue-gray pubescence	•									Sp	•			
Rhus typhina 'Dissecta' Deeply divided leaflets give the foliage a finely textured appearance	•	•		•							•	•		•
Robinia pseudoacacia 'Frisia' Brilliant golden-yellow leaves stand out even at a distance		•		•	•	•								
Salix magnifica Large leaves that may be mistaken for those of a magnolia			•							Sp				
Taxus baccata 'Standishii' Golden yellow leaves arranged radially on the shoots	•	•		•		•	•	•			•			•
Trachycarpus fortunei Fan-shaped leaves provide an unusual combination of shape and pattern				•				•		Su	•			•

KEY

Sp *spring* ■ **Su** *summer* ■ **F** *fall* ■ **W** *winter*

Fall color

Many trees give a flourish of leaf color in fall. The breakdown of the dominant green pigment chlorophyll reveals a range of other colored chemicals that may, in a good year, provide a glorious pallet of tones. Some trees can be relied on year-in, year-out, while others are more variable depending on weather conditions and may shed their leaves with little more than a slight yellowing. Japanese maples are perhaps the best-known trees for fall interest, many cultivars having been specially selected for their intense color. Though less renowned, many species of *Euonymus* give early leaf color in combination with their spectacular fruit.

NAME/DESCRIPTION	tolerates heavy clay soils	tolerates alkaline soils	tolerates poorly drained soils	tolerates dry soils	tolerates salt spray	tolerates exposure	tolerates extreme cold	evergreen	compact size	attractive flowers (season)	attractive fruit or cones	foliage interest	attractive bark	winter interest
Acer griseum Leaves turn an array of bright colors through red and orange													●	●
Acer japonicum 'Vitifolium' In fall leaves color to a deep red										Sp	●	●	●	
Acer palmatum 'Osakazuki' Fiery red fall leaves make this one of the best Japanese maples												●		
Amelanchier lamarckii Leaves provide color when newly open and again in fall	●		●							Sp				
Cercis canadensis Leaves often turn attractive tones of yellow		●		●						Sp	●			
Cladrastis kentukea Large pinnate leaves turn in fall to bright clear yellow	●	●										●		
Cornus kousa In the fall the leaves turn to glorious tones of red and orange										Su	●			
Cotinus coggygria The turning leaves provide a blaze of color		●								Su		●		
Crataegus crus-galli Leaves renowned for their fine range of fall colors	●		●	●	●	●	●			Sp	●			●
Eucryphia glutinosa Deciduous leaves often color to various shades of orange and red								s		Su				
Euonymus hamiltonianus Leaves color yellow and red in fall	●	●	●	●	●	●	●		●		●			
Euptelea polyandra Shapely leaves give excellent fall colors of red and yellow		●							●	Sp		●		
Lagerstroemia x *fauriei* Leaves often provide good range of fall color				●					●	Su/F			●	
Nyssa sinensis Fall colors from yellow through red and orange to purple				●								●	●	
Oxydendrum arboretum Glossy leaves turn to yellow, red, and purple										Su		●		
Parrotia persica Color starts early and turns the crown to red, yellow, and orange	●	●								W		●	●	●
Pyrus calleryana 'Bradford' Renowned for its fine fall color of bright orange and red				●						Sp				
Rhus typhina Large downy leaves turn deep orange	●	●		●							●	●		
Stewartia sinensis Unpredictable leaf color from bright red to orange										Su			●	●
Tilia mongolica Leaves end the year by turning a beautiful golden yellow							●							

KEY

Sp *spring* ■ **Su** *summer* ■ **F** *fall* ■ **W** *winter*

s *semi evergreen*

Clockwise from top left:
Acer davidii 'Serpentine'
Acer griseum
Arbutus unedo
Betula utilis
     var. *jacquemontii*
Parrotia persica
Lagerstroemia indica x
     fauriei
Pinus sylvestris 'Aurea'
Prunus serrula
Center:
Taxus baccata

Attractive bark

Ornamental bark is one of the most valuable of all assets in a garden tree. It can be used in a similar way to dramatic foliage to provide visual highlights, and trees should be carefully positioned for best effect. Some species, such as snake-bark maples, improve with age while others, notably willows, rely on repeated cutting to produce young brightly colored shoots. The pale-barked birches are particularly effective when grown in small groups in prominent positions. The bark of some trees is very tactile as well as visually attractive and may be positioned close to paths or paved areas where it can be best appreciated. An occasional stroke can help to clean algae and dirt off smooth-barked trees, giving them a beautiful gloss.

NAME/DESCRIPTION	tolerates heavy clay soils	tolerates alkaline soils	tolerates poorly drained soils	tolerates dry soils	tolerates salt spray	tolerates exposure	tolerates extreme cold	evergreen	compact size	attractive flowers (season)	attractive fruit or cones	foliage interest	fall color	winter interest
Acer davidii ssp. *grosseri* Striking gray-green bark with a fine patterning of white veins										Sp	●	●		
Acer griseum Rusty-brown bark peels in thin flakes to reveal differently colored underlayers													●	
Acer palmatum 'Sango kaku' Young shoots and stems brightly colored coral pink												●	●	●
Aralia elata Thick stems conspicuously covered in sharp spines	●	●	●							Su/F	●	●		
Arbutus unedo Roughly textured red-brown bark contrasts with shiny evergreen leaves		●		●	●		●			A	●			●
Betula utilis var. *jacquemontii* Striking bark varies from pure white through orange-brown to a deep copper	●						●							
Eucalyptus parvifolia Bark peels irregularly to reveal a range of colored layers beneath	●	●		●		●						●		
Lagerstroemia indica x *fauriei* Peeling bark attractively mottled in a variety of colors				●					●	Su/F			●	
Ligustrum lucidum Older trees often develop an attractively fluted trunk	●	●	●							Su/F				
Maackia amurensis Bark of young trees a rich shiny brown, becoming coarser and peeling with age		●								Su	●			
Morus nigra Bark soon becomes ruggedly contorted adding to the tree's aged character		●										●		
Nyssa sinensis Gray-brown bark cracks and flakes with age				●								●	●	
Parrotia persica Flaking bark develops a dappled pattern reminiscent of London plane	●	●								W		●	●	●
Pinus sylvestris 'Aurea' Variously colored bark peels in irregular plates	●		●	●	●	●	●				●			●
Prunus maackii Amber-colored glossy bark often flakes in large sheets	●	●					●			Sp				●
Prunus serrula Trunk and main limbs display superb glossy red-brown bark with peeling bands	●	●								Sp				
Salix alba 'Britzensis' Regularly pruned trees produce dazzling flame-red stems	●		●	●		●								
Stewartia pseudocamellia Red-brown bark flakes to reveal pink and gray underlayers				●						Su			●	
Syringa reticulata Shiny chestnut-brown bark with horizontal lenticels has a cherry-like appearance	●	●					●			Sp/Su				
Taxus baccata Mature trees develop attractively fluted and ridged red-brown bark	●	●		●	●	●		●			●			●

KEY

SP *spring* ■ **SU** *summer* ■ **F** *fall* ■ **W** *winter*

Clockwise from top left:
Betula utilis 'Silver Shadow'
Cedrus atlantica
    'Glauca Pendula'
Chamaecyparis pisifera
    'Filifera Aurea'
Cornus mas
Parrotia persica
Pinus sylvestris 'Aurea'
Salix alba 'Britzensis'
Salix daphnoides 'Aglaia'
Center:
Taxus baccata 'Standishii'

Winter interest

Trees with winter interest can be used to make gardens colorful and interesting even at the most unpromising time of year. The most obvious candidates are evergreens, particularly those with bright or variegated foliage such as the hollies. However, other features such as colored bark or ornamental branching pattern are just as valuable. A few species, among them *Cornus mas* and *Parrotia persica*, flower during late winter, welcome harbingers of spring to come. With a little planning, winter-interest plants can be grouped to maximize their impact in particular parts of the garden where they can be seen from a warm indoor vantage point.

NAME/DESCRIPTION	tolerates heavy clay soils	tolerates alkaline soils	tolerates poorly drained soils	tolerates dry soils	tolerates salt spray	tolerates exposure	tolerates extreme cold	evergreen	compact size	attractive flowers (season)	attractive fruit or cones	foliage interest	fall color	attractive bark
Arbutus unedo Urn-shaped white flowers and larger red fruits last into winter		●			●	●		●		F	●			●
Betula pendula 'Youngii' Winter sunlight gives the leafless crown a beautiful purple tinge	●		●	●	●	●	●							●
Betula utilis 'Silver Shadow' One of the most striking of all the white-barked birches	●						●							●
Cedrus atlantica 'Glauca Pendula' Pendulous branches hang to the ground to form a curtain of blue-gray foliage	●	●						●			●	●		
Chamaecyparis obtusa 'Nana Gracilis' Unusual fern-like sprays of glossy green foliage	●	●	●	●				●	●			●		
Chamaecyparis pisifera 'Filifera Aurea' Thread-like texture of foliage emphasized by its golden coloration	●	●	●	●			●	●				●		
Cornus mas Small yellow flowers pack the dense network of branches in late winter	●	●	●				●			W	●		●	
Crataegus x *lavelli* 'Carrierei' Leaves and fruits give good fall color that lasts well into winter	●	●	●		●	●	●			Sp	●		●	
Eucalyptus gunnii Ornamental bark and evergreen foliage provide winter color	●	●		●				●				●		●
Fagus sylvatica 'Purpurea Pendula' Winter's absence of leaves reveals a basket-like network of branches		●			●	●						●	●	
Ilex aquifolium Prickly evergreen leaves and bright shiny berries	●	●	●		●			●			●			
Juniperus scopulorum Strong symmetrical outline and evergreen foliage provide all-season interest	●	●				●	●	●						
Parrotia persica Bright red flowers appear in late winter and combine with dappled bark	●	●								W		●	●	●
Pinus sylvestris 'Aurea' In mid-winter the needles take on a glorious golden tone		●		●	●	●	●	●			●	●		●
Rhus typhina Dense panicles of hairy red fruits often persist right through the winter	●	●		●							●	●	●	
Robinia pseudoacacia 'Tortuosa' Contorted branches at their most dramatic in the winter		●		●	●		●					●		
Salix alba var. *vitellina* Golden yellow young stems best encouraged by regular pruning	●	●		●	●		●							●
Salix daphnoides 'Aglaia' Impressive bright yellow catkins and red shoots in winter	●	●		●			●			Sp				●
Taxus baccata (cultivars) Cultivars display a variety of colored and textured evergreen foliage	●	●		●		●		●			●	●		
Ulmus glabra 'Camperdownii' Pale winter branches form a weeping dome	●	●							●					

KEY

SP *spring* ■ **SU** *summer* ■ **F** *fall* ■ **W** *winter*

Further reading/Resources

Further reading

Conifers: The Illustrated Encyclopedia (2 Volumes)
by D. M. Van Gelderen, J. R. P. Van Hoey Smith
Publisher: Timber Press (OR); Updated edition
(October 1, 1996)

Crapemyrtle, A Grower's Thoughts
by David Byers
Publisher: Owl Bay Publishers; (July 1, 1997)

Diseases of Trees and Shrubs
by Wayne A. Sinclair, Howard H. Lyon, Warren T. Johnson
Publisher: Comstock Publishing; (July 1, 1987)

Hollies: The Genus Ilex
by Fred C Galle
Publisher: Timber Press (1997)

Japanese Maples
by J. D. Vertrees, Peter Gregory
Publisher: Timber Press; 3rd Rev edition (May 15, 2001)

Maples for Gardens: A Color Encyclopedia
by C.J. van Gelderen, D.M. van Gelderen
Publisher: Timber Press (OR); (September 1, 1999)

*Pests and Diseases: The Complete Guide to Preventing,
Identifying and Treating Plant Problems* (AHS Guides).
by Pippa Greenwood, Andrew Halstead, Chase A. R.,
Daniel Gilrein
Publisher: Dorling Kindersley Publishing; 1st edition
(February 1, 2000)

Pruning & Training (AHS Practical Guides)
by Christopher Brickell, David Joyce
Publisher: DK Publishing Inc; 1st American edition
(August 1, 1996)

The pruning of trees, shrubs and conifers
by George E Brown, Tony Kirkham, Roy Lancaster.
Publisher: Timber Press (OR); 2nd Rv&Enl edition
(February 1, 2004)

The Tree Doctor: A Guide to Tree Care and Maintenance
by Daniel Prendergast, Erin Predergast
Publisher: Firefly Books Ltd; (June 1, 2003)

Resources

American Horticultural Society
www.ahs.org
7931 East Boulevard Drive, Alexandria, VA 22308
The AHS is the oldest national gardening organization in the
country and members enjoy a range of benefits.

International Society of Arboriculture
www.isa-arbor.com
P.O. Box 3129, Champaign, IL 61826
The society produces a list of certified arborists and provides
advice on arboricultural matters.

The Maple Society
www.ubcbotanicalgarden.org/maplesociety
The Society was founded to cater for and foster interest
in maples.

American Association of Botanical Gardens and Arboreta
www.aabga.org
100 W 10th St Ste 614, Wilmington DE 19801
The association produces a list of hundreds of member
gardens and arboreta all over the USA and Canada.

United States Department of Agriculture
www.usda.gov
www.invasivespecies.gov
For information on diseases and invasive species.

The National Tree Trust
www.nationaltreetrust.org
Tree Link
www.treelink.org
For advice and information on creating a better environment
within your community with trees.

Westonbirt—The National Arboretum, Tetbury, Gloucestershire,
GL8 8QS, UK
www.forestry.gov.uk/westonbirt
Bedgebury—The National Pinetum, Park Lane, Goudhurst,
Cranbrook, Kent TN17 2SL, UK
www.forestry.gov.uk/bedgebury
The Forestry Commission's two national tree collections each
with outstanding collections of trees and shrubs.

Index

Page numbers in **bold** refer to main entries.
Page numbers in *italics* refer to captions.

Credits

Quarto would like to thank and acknowledge the following for supplying photographs reproduced in this book:

(Key: l left, r right, c center, t top, b bottom)

27	Nikhilesh Haval
72tl	Peter Stiles/Hortipix
72tr	Chris B Stock/Science Photo Library
72b	Wolfgang Kaehler/Corbis
83tl	Maurice Nimmo/Science Photo Library
83b	Adrian Thomas/Science Photo Library
92t	Irene Windridge/Science Photo Library
92c	Lance Beacham/Science Photo Library
92b	Kevin Fleming/Corbis
93t	Pam Collins/Science Photo Library
93b	William A. Bake/Corbis
123	GardenWorld Images
135t	Lynn Keddie/Garden Picture Library
135b	Geoff Kidd/Science Photo Library
141bl	Mike Comb/Science Photo Library
141br	John Glover/DK Images
142bl	GardenWorld Images
142br	Chris B Stock/Science Photo Library
143	GardenWorld Images
146t	Hans-Otto Tengrud/Camera Arborea Stock
146b	OSF/photolibrary.com
147	Joseph Strauch/DK Images
160bl	Irene Windridge/Science Photo Library
160br	Peter Stiles/Hortipix
168bc	William A. Bake/Corbis

Steve Wooster would like to thank the following: Westonbirt Arboretum; Dan Luscombe at Bedgebury National Pinetum; Hilliers Arboretum; RHS Gardens, Wisley; Kew Gardens; Chris Allhusen at Bradenham Hall Farms; John Brookes at Denhams; Luciano Giubbilei; Sir Miles Warren, Governor's Bay, New Zealand; Peter Cave's Tree Nursery, Pukeroro, New Zealand.

Author Acknowledgments

I would like to thank the following people and organizations for their help in the writing of this book:

The Forestry Commission at Westonbirt Arboretum and Bedgebury Pinetum. The inspiration for many of the species came from these two collections. In particular, Hugh Angus, Penny Jones, and Daniel Luscombe who helped with locating plants for photographing. Thanks also to the staff at Quarto Publishing for giving me the opportunity to write the book and the support during its production.

All other illustrations and photographs are the copyright of Quarto Publishing plc. While every effort has been made to credit contributors, Quarto would like to apologize should there have been any omissions or errors—and would be pleased to make the appropriate correction for future editions of the book.

Hardiness zones

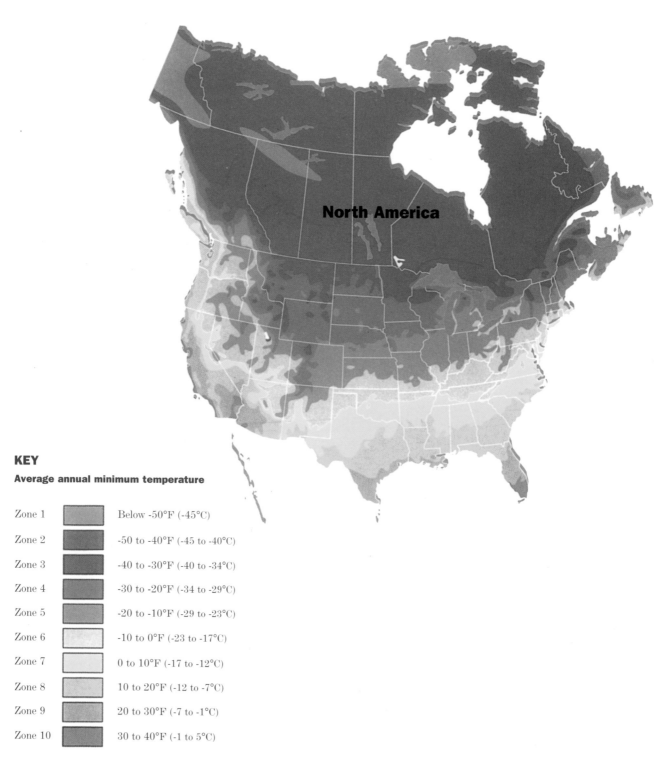

North America

KEY

Average annual minimum temperature

Zone	Temperature
Zone 1	Below -50°F (-45°C)
Zone 2	-50 to -40°F (-45 to -40°C)
Zone 3	-40 to -30°F (-40 to -34°C)
Zone 4	-30 to -20°F (-34 to -29°C)
Zone 5	-20 to -10°F (-29 to -23°C)
Zone 6	-10 to 0°F (-23 to -17°C)
Zone 7	0 to 10°F (-17 to -12°C)
Zone 8	10 to 20°F (-12 to -7°C)
Zone 9	20 to 30°F (-7 to -1°C)
Zone 10	30 to 40°F (-1 to 5°C)

Remember that hardiness is not just a question of minimum temperatures. A plant's ability to survive certain temperatures is affected by many factors, such as the amount of shelter given and its position within your garden.